The Small Company Pilot

In memory of DMB

The Small Company Pilot

A company survival guide

STEPHEN BLOOMFIELD

ICSA Publishing
The Official Publishing Company of
The Institute of Chartered Secretaries and Administrators

In association with

Prentice Hall Europe

London   New York   Toronto   Sydney   Tokyo   Singapore
Madrid   Mexico City   Munich   Paris

First published 1998 by
ICSA Publishing Limited
Campus 400, Maylands Avenue
Hemel Hempstead
Hertfordshire, HP2 7EZ

Typeset in 11/12pt Baskerville by
Hands Fotoset, Ratby, Leicester

Printed and bound in Great Britain by
MPG Books Ltd, Bodmin, Cornwall

British Library Cataloguing in Publication Data

A catalogue record for this book is available from
the British Library

ISBN 1-87-286091-5 (pbk)

1 2 3 4 5   02 01 00 99 98

Contents

Acknowledgements

I have been very fortunate in having had the opportunity to practise at first hand the use of the techniques which I have written about in this book. Those opportunities would not have arisen, nor developed the way that they did, but for the help, patience and support of many people.

Among those, I am particularly indebted to John Mardon, who led by example and whose own hard-bought experiences he has readily shared with me over a number of years. Bob Henry, Caroline Owens and their colleagues at Midland Growth Capital have also offered much support and practical help. David Wansbrough at ECI Ventures offered encouragement; I learned much from the people he put me in contact with. I am also very grateful to Maurice Moses, and his colleagues, at Levy Gee for their technical advice on several occasions. Although I would not have completed this book without the help of all these people, I would not expect them to agree with all that I have written; the opinions expressed in it are mine alone.

This book has stolen time from my wife, Gillian, and children, Philip and Kathleen, while I completed it. I have learned a great deal from them, too.

Stephen Bloomfield
1997

Introduction
'Alone, small and lonely'

This small book is intended as a primer for those engaged in the fraught activity of attempting to salvage businesses which have fallen on difficult times. It is essentially a practical book rather than an academic work, intended to indicate strategies that can be put into action rather than to be an extended dissertation on the theoretical management principles behind them. People in trouble don't have time to read extended tracts on the latest management theory – they want quick help and, possibly, some comfort that someone else has been through the same problems before them.

As an introduction to some of the strategies that have worked in practice in cases where businesses have been in deep distress, it is born out of personal experience and the tested experience of others – and experience inevitably is developed through the application of ideas, the making of mistakes and the occasional failure. Not all businesses that need help to recover are in *deep* distress of course. Some just need a sustained period of detailed attention by someone who knows better than the incumbent management how the business should be run. In these circumstances, the information contained in the various chapters can be diluted to taste. But it seems that the best thing for an author on recoveries to do is to assume that the worst is what potential readers will want to know how to deal with so that they can pick out appropriate suggestions which come closest to matching the situations they face.

The analogy that is usually employed in describing the process of salvage of a business in distress is that of doctoring. This has unelaborated images accompanying it of a slightly distanced clinical professional who looks at symptoms, riffles through the mental pages of their extensive knowledge, diagnoses the ill, then suggests and applies a cure.

This seems to me to an analogy more appropriate to the larger company where time and resources *may* be under slightly less pressure

1

than in the rough and tumbled, less polished world of the small to medium-size business. In the large company environment, if the patient does not recover then the outcome is unfortunate, regrettable too of course, and may be extremely costly in jobs and in financial terms too – but it is not, usually, terminal for the doctor as well.

I used to work for a financial organisation run by a man who has since risen to a very eminent position and was very fond of saying that successful businesses were all about three things: 'Management, management and management'. I didn't agree with him then and I don't agree with him now. Successful businesses – and the recovery of previously successful businesses that have fallen on hard times – do depend on a combination of three things, admittedly. But these have to be the right proportions of Money, Market and Management.

Recovering a company, turning it round to profits, requires reviving and controlling these factors – with the added contribution of a large dollop of luck along the way. It also requires some nerve and a healthy quantity of self-confidence, together with the ability to assimilate information fast and make rapid assessments based on partial and shifting information. To my mind the whole process is more than a bit like flying an aeroplane and the process of recovery is like catching an aeroplane out of a sudden manoeuvre and bringing it back to straight and level flight.

In the small company environment the manager charged with the rescue has much greater involvement with the practicalities of the situation. The situation is less akin to the calm of the consulting room than the confines of the cockpit of a small plane, where the things done – or not done – by the pilot will have a profound effect on his own well-being; where information is sometimes conflicting; and where forces outside the control of the pilot occasionally make life more difficult than any self-induced action.

There is a small number of very good books available that describe how to turn around loss-making companies into profit. Unfortunately for the majority of managers of businesses in this country, most of these books treat the exercise from the point of view of someone dropped into loss-making businesses under the wing of a large parent company.

Most businesses in this country are not like that. Most are small independent businesses, owner-managed or run by a small management team directly rather than through a complicated subsidiary–parent relationship. But most businesses find themselves in some sort of turmoil at some stage in their lives, either financial or organisational and usually both at the same time.

This book tries to do something different from the texts that cater for the subsidiaries and groups, in looking at the remedies available to the manager of the small to medium-size independent company with cash problems. In other words, the owner or manager of a business that finds itself crucially dependent upon its own resources for survival – by stemming the outflow of cash, changing ways of operation and somehow, in the longer term, filling the hole in the balance sheet left by trading losses. It assumes only a limited grounding in formal business theory – the approach taken is a step-by-step consideration of the process of recovery.

The type of company that this book is likely to be of value to has the following profile:

- turning over up to £5m annually;
- in existence for at least three years;
- employing up to 50 people;
- has no parent company that can bail it out;
- has experienced serious losses over a relatively short period of time, or lower levels of loss over a more prolonged period but has previously been profitable;
- is experiencing problems in paying its creditors within the time previously regarded as normal;
- has a nervous banker who is reluctant to extend further overdraft facilities or anxious to reduce existing levels of overdraft;
- has a relatively small number of shareholders.

The book does not set out to be a blueprint for survival for such companies. There is no such thing. It does set out to explain some of the methods which might be used to bring companies back from the brink at a time when the managers in them face sustained pressure from bankers and creditors.

But a word of warning is necessary. Reading the book and trying to apply the suggestions in it cannot, by itself, ensure that survival will come about. Inevitably the book deals in generalities; managers under pressure need specifics. Unfortunately for those who want ready-made solutions to a problem, every case is different when dealing with people. The infuriating thing about case studies is that they never quite match your own situation – and you can waste a lot of time leafing through management manuals trying to find the case that exactly corresponds to your situation.

But conclusions about certain actions that are appropriate in a situation can be drawn from basic principles . This is what the book will seek to do, to draw out the basic principles of attacking certain problems in order to allow the method to be applied in other circumstances. The method of doing this will be to apply experience from real cases where appropriate, together with the employment of a particular analogy – comparing running a business to flying an aeroplane.

But even applying the book's suggestions rigorously cannot

guarantee results. There are always a number of different ways of tackling a problem, some of which will offer better chances than others, and as in any business venture, a fair amount of luck is required for success. The solution will be the right one if it works and it will be the wrong one if it doesn't; there is no other test.

But as with everything else, the harder you work the luckier you seem to get. (And in this context, as we shall see, working harder does not necessarily mean working longer. It means getting more out of every hour of effort – both on your part and, even more importantly, on the part of others.)

At the least, though, reading the book and absorbing and applying the information in it may contribute to making sure that your company never enters the 'circle of confusion' characterised by falling margins, by red ink on the P&L account, by increasing levels of overdraft and lengthening creditor days. In this respect, the book may also be of value to bankers and advisers to companies, as well as to managers who want to avoid the problems described.

There are three main themes that run through the principles described in the book:

• the value of leadership;
• the efficient and effective use of time;
• the harnessing of common sense.

Around these three themes is grouped a fluid arrangement of others: the effective use of people; the imposition of sensible systems of operation in times of organisational stress; the need for the ability to take decisive and effective action at speed; and the need for openness and fairhandedness (or as much as can be afforded in the circumstances). All these subordinate factors are reducible to one, eventually – the need to be organised. Not organised in the facile sense of carrying a bulging Filofax around – although that may help if it is properly employed – but in the more basic sense of knowing, absolutely clearly, four things:

• what you are doing;
• why you are doing it;
• what you need to do next;
• and what you need to do after that.

The restoration of a company to financial health has become known as 'company doctoring' – for obvious reasons. But in truth, the activities involved have less affinity with the sophistication of modern medicine than with the practices of the barber surgeons of two and three hundred years ago. The recovery process can be bloody, very painful, very messy and unpleasant. The subject of the attention probably survives – as they did two hundred years ago – more because of the basic strength of the constitution than because of the outright skill of the doctor.

As suggested above, a better metaphor might be borrowed from flying. Piloting an aeroplane involves physically exercising control and making continual adjustments rather than prescribing pills and potions and watching the results. It can involve moments of confusion and sweaty-palmed uncertainty rather than clinical order. (And it often involves leaps of the intuitive rather than the rational.)

There are three basic requirements which all fledgling pilots are taught, to be followed in sequence in order to keep things working the way that they should. The priority order of activity is 'Aviate; Navigate; Communicate'. In other words, maintain control and keep flying, plot your path and tell others where you are going – in that order.

The same order of priority is probably appropriate for turning a company away from financial problems. The most important thing to do is to keep flying – keep the company up and running, anticipating the continuous problems of control that you are going to meet while the wind buffets you. At the same time, try to reduce your workload – try to arrange your activities in such a way that you are able to anticipate the next problem rather than let a continuous stream of problems control you. Trainee pilots are told to 'get ahead of the aeroplane' – in other words to anticipate their next set of actions and the likely consequences – rather than to wait for the next problem to arise.

Next, make sure that you know where you are going minute by minute (both for your own purposes to get to your destination and to make sure that you don't hit any further problems).

Lastly, let people know what you are doing so that they can help.

The superiority of the aviation analogy over the medical analogy is that it also provides a philosophy for looking after the company when things have begun to right themselves, and therefore it is more appropriate to the process of control of a company by an owner-manager than the doctoring approach. You (normally) only go to a doctor when you are ill but a pilot has to keep flying all the time. And if the analogy is extended to a crew (a managerial team) rather than a single individual then the relationship between metaphor and real world becomes even more apt.

The very first thing to do is to be certain who is in command. After that comes determining the state of the business – the commercial equivalents of finding out how many engines are still working; how much fuel is left; how many passengers are on board (you should be carrying freight not passengers!).

When you are sure that you are still aviating, then you can turn your attention to navigating – plotting a course for recovery and avoiding the next patch of high ground. In the case of a business the navigational data are triple-faceted, dealing with the areas of management, money and market.

Once the course has been worked out the next thing to do is to implement it. The new course also has to take into account that the original information coming to the managers was probably inadequate in some way or other, so the navigational data have to be updated continually and adjustments made to the course plotted to take into account the business equivalents of wind drift and fuel availability.

Next comes communicating your intentions and finding out what others are doing. The four audiences that you have to consider are bankers, creditors, customers and the workforce – and shareholders, too, if you are not in sole control. In aviation terms these might be equivalent to fuel tankers, cargo, passengers and the aircraft's owners – make your own mind up which is which. They all have a right to know what is going on at some point, but they do not necessarily need the same information or at the same time.

But there are added complications at this stage which have to be dealt with, equivalent in aviating terms to 'other traffic'. It is not too difficult to imagine at times that bankers, creditors and customers are all trying to be Baron von Richthofen – all trying to manoeuvre themselves into a position where they can shoot you down.

Dealing with bankers is an art in itself – in aviating terms it comes under the heading of advanced aerobatics. Too often, many of the problems that companies find themselves in have been caused by over-aggressive lending on the part of banks. Harsh attitudes towards companies which have got into trouble, and which need some time and understanding to sort themselves out rather than further aggressive handling, then compound the problem. To be fair though, the understandable dilemma that bankers face is that 'understanding' often translates into 'additional cash' – in other words, a usually unacceptable request for them to extend their risk again.

At times, when the needs of a number of parties have to be considered and co-ordinated, air traffic control has to be consulted for instructions: the rules of the air have to be observed. In business terms a specialist sometimes ought to be asked for a view on the legitimacy of continuing trading and the prospects of formal insolvency. Sometimes these opinions will bring about the end of any further activity – aerial or otherwise.

But assuming that you manage to recover control, once you are in clear air, knowing where you are going and able to recognise the intentions of other traffic, you can begin to repeat the last two stages of the cycle: you can keep aviating all the time while making minor navigational adjustments continually to keep on track and communicating as appropriate to let others know of your position and intentions.

Chapter 1

Pilot in command

Rules of the air

It may be only a minor bending of the truth to say that the natural state of most small businesses is one of imminent collapse. That provocative statement needs explaining, since manifestly there are some very prosperous small businesses – and big businesses grow from small businesses that have successfully made the progression from small to medium and then to something larger still without collapsing.

The point that I am making, in saying that small businesses continually live in danger of collapse, is that the line between success and disaster for most small businesses is very thin, since they lack the financial and managerial resources which larger businesses can call on to protect themselves in times of adversity. Any destabilising moment will have a severe effect on the fortunes of a small company. Hitting a pocket of financial turbulence can be a major problem for a small company while it would only faze a large business temporarily. Usually a small business is kept going by the hard work and ability of a small core of managers; and usually the cash backing for the small business is fairly meagre – since otherwise they would be bigger businesses.

So most small and medium-size businesses spend a good part of their time and resources effectively defying gravity – a bit like an aeroplane flying through the air, buffeted by the power of forces greater than itself, in danger from moment to moment of falling out of the air unless it keeps on flying.

Most people have some appreciation that the flight of an aeroplane is governed by rules, both physical laws which suggest what will happen in a situation where different forces act on the plane, and 'rules of the air' which control the pilot's conduct of the aeroplane in terms of what should be done to ensure safe passage through the sky. Some of these are, effectively, good advice based on the experience of others; some of the rules control the way the pilot is obliged to behave.

The conduct of a business is also governed by rules. Some of the rules are explicit and codified, others are implicit and 'understood'; some are formal and have the backing of society through the force of law, others are adhered to voluntarily because it makes life easier.

If the rules which govern the running of a business – legal, economic, financial, cultural, social – are followed, then the business will probably prosper. If they are ignored, then inevitably in time the business will falter and may collapse. The same holds true for flying aeroplanes: if the rules of flying – both the physical laws and the man-made rules – are obeyed then the aeroplane keeps flying and reaches its destination. If not, it crashes. The analogy that running a business is a bit like flying a plane seems to hold in this area, too.

The purpose of this book is to try to demonstrate some of the rules that have to be obeyed when a business has got into difficulty, so that it can be recovered as a viable source of value for its shareholders, managers, customers, suppliers and employees. The way in which this will be done is to use the analogy already outlined – of an aeroplane flying through the air, proceeding on its way to its destination, carrying cargo and fuel and defying gravity.

The first part of this process of applying the analogy then is to establish some of the 'rules of the air' that need to be observed in considering why and how a plane flies.

A plane will fly if the sum of the lift forces that are applied to it is greater than the sum of the drag forces applied to it. Other factors act on the aeroplane at times – head winds, bad visibility, turbulence and storms – and tend to push it off course. These need to be allowed for in setting the course for the destination. Similar allowances have to be made in running a business: plans have to be adjusted as different factors bear upon the initial plan. In the case of a business the components of lift are profit and cashflow – and of these, the greater is cashflow – while drag is debt, costs of manufacture and taxes.

However, while a plane flies because the sums of the interaction of forces that are applied to it are greater in one direction than in another, the interactions of these forces are controlled and applied by the pilot. If the pilot does not pay enough attention to what is going on then the aeroplane does not fly smoothly or drifts off the course originally set. The pilot's inputs are crucial. The same will be true for a business. The business manager has to understand the situation and make adjustments to the way that the business runs by trimming the controls that are applied to the business.

Usually for a plane in ordinary conditions, these trimming inputs are small adjustments. When things get out of hand, larger inputs have to be applied and the physical burden of flying becomes more tiring. Then the pilot might share some of the cockpit workload with a co-pilot. But even so the distinction between the responsibilities of the two is very clear.

It is a fundamental rule of the air that there can be only one pilot in command of an aeroplane. The reasons for this are obvious: it would be very dangerous to have two or more people trying to decide independently on courses of action or debating whether to turn left or right and making different inputs to the controls; at best, if it did not crash, the aircraft would never get to its destination but would meander aimlessly around the sky – unless one pilot made decisions that the other always agreed with. (This does not mean that pilot and co-pilot do not consult each other nor does it mean that the recovery manager should press ahead on a course of action without consulting the crew, of course.)

The same haphazard progress would be true for a business in trouble if no coherent plan were established by which the business could be driven or if every decision about the course to be taken were to be arrived at by means of a vote.

So the most important rule to be followed as far as decision-making is concerned is that *there should be only one person in overall command* of a recovering business, just as there can be only one pilot in overall command in an aeroplane. It is of critical importance when you start the recovery of a business in trouble that you ensure that you have the authority to get things done, as and when you want them done, and that you have the authority to make the necessary changes in the business that will bring about recovery.

Without this authority all your good ideas about how to salvage the business will come to nothing: intelligence and ability are impotent without an effective means of application. If there is someone behind you or above you – a shareholder, another director or adviser – counter-manding your decisions then you are quite simply wasting your time in trying to salvage the business. What is worse, you are probably placing yourself in jeopardy by being nominally in control of the business when the actual control lies elsewhere. You will be in the unfortunate position of having the responsibility for what happens when you do not have the authority to make sure that what you want to have happen gets done. In these situations, if you cannot bring your authority to bear to eliminate the managerial opposition, the proper course of action is to bail out and leave the direction of the recovery to the individual whose decisions are conflicting with yours. This may be a hard choice to make and have difficult consequences, but there is no margin in trying to salvage the unsalvageable.

Unfortunately, the situation where there is a conflicting source of authority is all too often encountered. People like interfering for all sorts of reasons: sometimes for power, sometimes for egotistical reasons, sometimes for money. Whatever the cause, time spent by the pilot in fighting the rest of the crew rather than the outside world is time wasted and it inhibits the execution of the main task of recovery, so the situation must be resolved as quickly as possible.

Leadership is a difficult thing to exercise at any time and more so when conditions are difficult. In the context of recovering a business, there are very powerful internal and external pressures on the recovery manager to perform to expectations and demonstrate a high degree of ability. As well as the internal self-generated desire to do a good job – a strong motivation or the responsibility would not have been accepted in the first place – there will be pressures from other members of the management, from shareholders, suppliers, creditors and, not least, from the bank. Some will be willing to put trust in the recovery manager and agree to being led because they are anxious to make sure that the recovery goes well since they have a lot to lose if it does not. Others will be willing to accept the leadership of someone who apparently has the ability to lead them out of the mire that they find themselves stuck in. Some others will have darker motives and will be watching carefully for any stumble or sign of poor judgement. In each of these cases, the *permission* to lead is granted on perpetual trial at the effective consent of the led. If things are to go well it is of vital importance then that the recovery manager maintains the trust of those to whom leadership is being given. Making a mistake once may just be forgiven if the results are not too serious and the situation can be put right at no great cost, but making several simple mistakes or the same one over again, or a large mistake that costs money, will not. 'More than any other medium the air is unforgiving of any minor mistake' – very much the same could be said for recovery management.

You will make mistakes during the recovery – that much is certain. But being able to recover from them is the real test and that requires the ability to think through the consequences of your actions and be ready for the next eventuality. So the next rule, the second in the catechism of the recovery manager, is *never suggest a course of action which you have not already thought out* – even if only in outline – for yourself. While at its simplest this means that you should not risk compromising your authority by taking leaps into the dark and making the same mistakes as the managers who brought the business low in the first place, it has far more significance than simply saving face and preserving self-esteem. Without a long-term plan and an objective – or, better still, a series of smaller 'milestone' objectives that lead logically to the final objective by assessable steps – decisions are taken simply in terms of localised expediency, bowing to the immediate pressures facing the business. The effect is the same as the aimless meanderings through the sky brought about by the controls being shared by different pilots.

The third rule is *establish a base line of information for yourself*. In order to pilot the business effectively, and to reach your destination safely, you have to know where you are starting from – as we shall see later in greater detail in Chapter 3 – since finding your way home is intimately linked to knowing where you are.

The fourth rule is that *once decisions are taken everyone abides by them*. While you may tolerate differences of opinion in your management team up to the point when decisions are reached – in fact you should encourage the expression of different views since that is the way to develop a sensible forward strategy – you should eliminate any dissent thereafter. Running a business is not a matter of canvassing everyone's views and taking the line of least resistance. A pilot does not turn to the co-pilot halfway through a nose-dive, with one engine on fire, the wings creaking with stress and the altimeter unwinding like a cartoon clock, and say, 'Well, Fred. Any preference? Gatwick or Heathrow?'

Simply not agreeing with the plan in the first place is not a good reason for a subordinate to want to change it. Decisions should be taken on the strength of the evidence and arguments that can be marshalled in favour of one option. The choice of one course of action over another implies that the evidence behind the discarded option was weaker than for the chosen option. Or perhaps, despite intrinsically strong evidence, one of the protagonists could not present their case adequately. Whatever the reason, once the choice is made then there should be no reworking of the argument. Remember the first rule: there is only one pilot in command.

There will undoubtedly be times when it is appealing to follow a line of argument because it may sweeten one of the key members of the management team. But be very wary of adopting a course of action because of any reason other than the argument behind it and the potential benefit that it will have on the recovery plan for the business. And never ever be caught by the adoption of a course of action that involves losing a cash advantage unless the payback period has been worked out very soundly.

All this effectively adds up to the fifth rule, the sum of all the others: *work to a plan*. Once you have adopted that plan, having thought through the implications and set milestones, there should be no going back unless the milestones are not being achieved and there is clear evidence that the plan is not working.

The plan is your map for getting out of the mess that you find yourself in and constructing that plan will be *the* major task that you tackle during the early stages of the recovery. Constructing it will become part of the recovery itself since in preparing the plan you will simultaneously be making alterations to the way that the business is run .

At its most basic that plan is to keep the business alive, develop a simple course for recovery and then to publicise the plan and the course. There is a simple and robust rule for the order of priority in which things must be done by a pilot. That rule says that first the pilot must keep the plane flying, then that the pilot must steer the plane towards its destination, and only when these things are done must the pilot tell others where the plane is going. The rule is abbreviated to a series of one-word instructions:

Aviate;
Navigate;
Communicate.

The recovery manager should follow those rules absolutely. The business – the plane – must be kept flying or everything else is pointless; however, there is no sense in simply flying unless you have a purpose or a destination. Only when you are sure that the first two rules are being observed can you tell other people where you are going. In fact, until then you should not tell others where you are going since you would be misleading them if you did.

Before we leave this subject there is another worthwhile skill that pilots have to develop which you ought to begin to cultivate and that is the skill (and discipline) of writing information down while you are doing other things. The pilot has to write down runway headings, radio frequencies, wind speed and direction and barometric readings while flying the plane – and usually has to do the writing while there are other pressing problems to be dealt with, such as lining up for landing, or changing headings while climbing out of an airfield control zone, or steering a course to avoid other aircraft. None of the things that you will be doing will be quite as pressing as that – and equally, to be fair, you will not be able to get away with the minimal information that the pilot has to record. But you should develop the habit of writing down some aspects of what you are doing as a matter of good discipline.

The extent to which you should do this will vary with the significance of what you are seeking to record, but you must make sure that all board meetings or meetings of directors are recorded quickly and accurately after the event; you probably should make notes of all conversations with your bank manager and auditors; you *must* make notes of any meetings with insolvency practitioners.

It is also a good discipline for your own purposes to distil the events of each week into some form of report – perhaps just for your own consumption – so that you are able to look back and consider what you have done and how you have performed over a given period.

Everyone learns by making mistakes. You must be careful that yours are not too serious. You can contribute to that by reviewing the effects of your actions at a later convenient date when their full effects have worked their way through the business.

There is another, apocryphal, rule of the air that is worth stating too. This says that the three most useless things in aviation are runway behind you, height above you and a tenth of a second earlier. Transpose 'runway' with profit and loss, replace 'height above you' with cash, keep the element of time where it is, and you have another very suitable piece of advice for running businesses as well.

Key points

1. The business will continue to fly only if the forces lifting it up are greater then the forces pulling it down. Of these forces the most significant one is cash.

2. The order of priority of action is Aviate, Navigate, Communicate.

3. You are working to a plan, and there are four rules to follow in achieving that plan:
    Rule 1: There is only one pilot in command;
    Rule 2: Think your actions through before you implement them;
    Rule 3: Establish a base line of information for yourself;
    Rule 4: Once decisions are taken everyone abides by them.

Chapter 2

Keeping flying

As we have seen, trainee pilots are taught that they have three tasks which are, in priority order, aviating, navigating and communicating. In truth the triple tasks are virtually indistinguishable in importance while an aeroplane is flying normally. The same is true for a business: planning the business's path and controlling its progress at the same time as telling colleagues, employees, customers and bankers what is going on are all essential activities that contribute to the continued well-being of the enterprise.

But once things go wrong in flight then the pilot has no option but to concentrate on the primary task of keeping the aeroplane in the air. Spending all the time in plotting a new course or telling air traffic control what is going on while the plane is in a spin is going to lead to worse trouble. Priorities tend to establish themselves on a simple basis.

Just as the most important task of the pilot in trouble is to keep airborne, the most important task of the manager in a troubled business is to keep the business going. (The very first task is not to get into the situation where you have to think only about one aspect of flying or doing business, of course – but knowing what you *should* have done in the first place is no real comfort in time of crisis.)

But big problems grow from insignificant beginnings, both in flying and in business. Just as failing to pay attention to wind drift can lead the plane far from the desired track without the pilot realising what is going on, so failure to recognise the beginnings of a business problem can bring about commercial disaster. Small problems are easier to correct while they are small than when they have been allowed to develop into big problems.

One of the major components of resolving any problem, though, is the process of identifying just what is going wrong. Time spent in analysing the root of a problem may seem like time wasted when the immediate reaction is that every moment counts in resolving difficulties. The desire to do something is a natural response of many practical managers to the presentation of a problem. But finding out the nature of the problem rather than just bashing at it reflexively is an essential first step in determining the best way to tackle it – the trick is to recognise just the right amount of time that needs to be spent in analysis without going too far into futile conjecture.

In combination with procedures described in the next chapter – which aims to provide a method of identifying how and when the company was brought to its current condition – an analysis of the symptoms is a crucial task for effecting a cure.

There are four easily identifiable symptoms of a company in trouble financially. Quite probably, there are others too, but four are enough to be going on with and any company with these four in full-blown or partially developed form is certainly in trouble. Finding more indicators for the fun of it then becomes an interesting exercise for academic minds rather than for those involved in working their way out of the situation.

The categorisation that is outlined below may seem crude and simplistic but at this stage all that is required is a broad-brush approach. Successively finer filters can then be applied to the basic analysis to help determine what needs to be done.

Each of the four major signposts is like a set of Russian dolls where each contains a smaller one nesting inside. The four major signposts are indications of further problems, and these in turn will have to be eliminated or investigated further.

Once the initial signpost/symptom has been identified, the question 'Why?' should be asked until there is no further answer possible that can be filleted by a further 'Why?' At that point, the root of the problem should be exposed.

Signpost 1 Falling turnover

By itself, falling turnover is not a problem – provided that the decline is only seasonal or short term and not too precipitate. If the company is sufficiently flexible and the management sufficiently nimble, variations in turnover pose only an irritation to efficient running rather than a threat to the company's existence. A gentle and short-lived decline may even conceivably be of benefit in shaking up a company's organisation, a mild jolt out of bad habits and organisational ruts.

But in combination with other immediately identifiable major symptoms, a sustained, rapid or accelerating fall in turnover is a deadly threat to a company. Reductions in turnover arise principally in two ways:

- because of fewer units of sales; or
- because the same number of sales is made but at lower prices per unit.

In each case the decline can be:

- as a consequence of a decline in market share;
- as a result of an absolute decline in the market that the company serves.

Categorising the reasons for the decline in turnover provides a basic indication of the remedial action that might be taken. As we shall see in another chapter, the categorisation might indicate that action has to be taken concerning product quality, product range, price or some form of competitive behaviour or that changes have to be made in the way that the product is sold or in the resources employed to sell it.

Signpost 2 Declining margins

Except in very rare cases, declining margins always presage a real problem, one that is going to be difficult and time-consuming to overcome. In the context of a company in trouble, falling margins are likely signposts to either a serious costing problem or a serious people problem. In both cases, the problem will cost a good deal of effort and is likely to take a considerable amount of time to put right.

Signpost 3 Longer lead times

In a manufacturing or project-based business, an increase in the amount of time taken to complete a job can mean one of three things. It is an indication of either:

- increasing complexity of the job; or
- design difficulties; or
- materials procurement problems.

All these bear further investigation as, once again, they are probably the sign of a deeper problem.

Almost inevitably, unplanned longer job times lead to declining margins. Accurately costing the input of time becomes increasingly difficult in a job that is complicated to perform. Additional unforeseen costs may have to be absorbed by a contract won at an immovable price: even contingency factors used to bulk up a price can be worn down as a result of the use of expensive labour that has not been provided for in estimating costs.

Work completed at nil or negative margin has the effect of further demoralising those involved in the execution of the task, leading to a vicious downward spiral of decay that goes back again to attack turnover, margins and cash.

Signpost 4   Extending creditor days

The surest outward sign that a company is in trouble is an extension in the number of days that it takes to pay suppliers. Not surprisingly, suppliers are extremely sensitive to this treatment and the problem may well become self-reinforcing. In other words, after a brief space when the company appears to have benefited from taking longer to pay, suppliers' attitudes will harden and the company may well find itself even more hard-pressed to pay its bills on time – making the overall problem even more difficult to overcome.

Suppliers will do one of four things in response to a unilateral extension of their terms of payment. In ascending order of hostility, they will:

- increase their prices to take account of the interest factor that they have to bear in not receiving their money on the due date;
- press for faster payment by ringing up, writing warning letters or, most unpleasantly, taking legal action;
- demand cash with order;
- cease trading with the offending company – inevitably usually at the most inconvenient time, when the component or service which they supply cannot be obtained from anywhere else within a reasonable time or at a reasonable price.

All these actions on the part of suppliers can be extremely disruptive and may jeopardise recovery if they happen at an untoward moment.

As we shall see later, the best thing that you can do is to try not to get into a situation where suppliers take defensive action against you. Usually some form of warning to suppliers of an inevitable delay in payment will help – provided their goodwill is not tested to breaking point – especially if your business is very important to them. But there are some creditors who cannot be put off in this way and these are inevitably the ones who can kill a company: the difficult ones are usually the Inland Revenue, the Customs and Excise and the bank. Dealing with these is covered in later chapters.

An extension of creditor days is, very obviously, an indication that there is more money going out of a business than is coming in. The managers are having to make choices about whom to pay on time to keep the business going. Money is not being recovered from customers as fast as it is being consumed by the business in payments to suppliers. For the company this could mean that

- there is an imbalance between large and small orders;
- turnover is falling;
- margins are decreasing;
- lead times for individual jobs are becoming longer.

In short, it is evident that we have arrived back at the beginning of the circle – which serves to emphasise the inter-relatedness of the symptoms. It also indicates that the only way to break the circle is to tackle the problems in a sensible, planned way by choosing the problem (or more likely problems) that can be most easily solved in the shortest time.

Doing that – choosing the target or targets for your immediate attention – can be done after determining how and when the company was brought to its crisis, which is the subject of the next chapter.

Key points

1. Reflexive bashing of a problem may seem both satisfying and a practical way of getting out of difficulty initially but it is no substitute for proper analysis. It also rapidly loses its attractions once it is proved to be ineffective – by which time the situation has probably deteriorated further.

2. Review the components of your difficulty to try to isolate what it is that is causing your problem; the four major symptoms are:

    falling turnover; declining margins; longer lead times; extending creditor days.

    Each of these suggests a different beginning to the basic problem but they may all be intertwined.

3. Ask the question 'Why?' until you get to what you think is the root of the problem(s).

4. Once you have discovered what you believe is the source of the problem then you can begin to apply corrective action.

Chapter 3

How did we get here?

Being lost is not a feeling that many people find comfortable. At its mildest it can produce feelings of unease – passing through anxiety and going all the way to panic, according to the seriousness of the situation. In a business in trouble, the feeling of not knowing where you are is deeply unsettling to all concerned – managers and shop-floor – and this almost always produces a corrosive demoralisation that colours all decisions and activities, bringing about a cycle of poor decisions and poor prospects.

From this, it follows that one of the first jobs of the manager who wants to turn around a failing company is to find out why the company got itself into its current position. This is the application of the second rule (the first, that there is only one pilot-in-command is one to which we shall return in the next chapter). Only if you know where you are can you hope to plot the right course to get to where you want to go. And knowing how you got to where you are is the first part of the process of doing that.

The problem is knowing where to start. A company in trouble all too often exhibits a number of features that make life difficult for anyone who wants to try to sort it out. Aside from the obvious – and serious – problems of staff morale and financial pressure, it is all too often the case that the basic information on which to base a recovery strategy is not available. So one of the primary tasks of anyone who is going to try to pull a company round is to establish what information is actually needed as the basis for some sensible business decisions.

The state of being lost has three components: the first is not knowing how you got to where you are; the second is not recognising the location you find yourself in; and the last is not knowing in which direction to travel to get to where you want to go. If those three components persist then you stay lost. If you break out of one of the components then you stop being lost. (You may not know precisely where you are but you begin to locate your position more closely than you could otherwise.) And since usually the only one you can hope to break out of – logically – in a business environment is not knowing how you got to where you are, that is the place to start.

Let us go back to the aviation analogy briefly. Partly out of arrogance and partly out of the discipline of a process of thought that acts as a shield against panic, flyers never admit to being lost. They may be 'temporarily uncertain of their position' but they are certainly never *lost*.

The same will be true for most companies: they may have become temporarily uncertain of where they are and where they should be going but most of them will have some appreciation of how they got to where they are. So, by our analysis of the state of being lost given above, they cannot really be described as 'lost'. Like flyers they are 'temporarily uncertain of their position'. By reviewing the events that brought them to where they now are, one of the components of being 'lost/temporarily uncertain' can be eliminated and the new course for recovery can be plotted from the position that is established.

How do you go about working out roughly where you are? With the exception of flight over trackless desert or over the sea, pilots who become 'temporarily uncertain' are told to:

1. stay calm (always stay calm!);
2. temporarily maintain current heading unless it is obviously wrong to do so;
3. establish a 'most probable area' where they think they might be;
4. scan their maps until they recognise a landmark (usually one that they have just passed); and then
5. set a new course to their destination from where they think they have located themselves as being.

The same sort of procedure, using the basic principles and changing the terms where necessary, is appropriate to finding a new course for a company that is in trouble.

Furthermore, the sequence adopted for pilots who are 'temporarily uncertain' is a good sequence for the manager of a distressed business to follow in more than one way. Like an aviator, it is not possible for a manager of a company to call a complete halt to activity in order to take stock of the situation. The aeroplane has to be kept flying and the company has to be kept running. A car driver can stop the car to consult a map or ask a passer-by for directions, but there are no road signs or lay-bys in the sky, just as there are no unambiguous direction signs at every junction where a business decision has to be taken.

So, the explanations of what has gone wrong have be derived while on the run and at the same time as the company is kept going – paying its way as best it can and keeping customers as happy as possible during a difficult time.

To repeat, the purpose of the first part of the recovery exercise is to stay calm. Thrashing around in a panic-stricken state will do no one any good and will make the situation worse. The way to approach the problem is to bring some order to the situation by approaching the difficulties rationally.

Then, unless it is obvious that what is being done is going to bring about the collapse of the company within a very short space of time – that means days rather than weeks – continue those practices that seem reasonable in the circumstances while you sort out what went wrong. This is the businesses equivalent of 'Maintain your current heading'.

Then try to establish the path that brought the company to its present position by scanning your maps. In a business sense, management information and accounts are the equivalent of aerial charts. Use the information available to you from the collection of management statistics used by the business to find out where you are and try to recognise a landmark from which you can base your recovery plan.

The best types of information to use for this purpose are the company's previous business plans; the statement of sources and uses of funds that accompany statutory accounts; and the monthly financial reviews that many banks ask for. If you are a new manager, brought in specifically to turn the business round, beware taking for granted the accuracy of the last of these and treat the other two with caution. All too often the information prepared for the bank will have been 'adjusted' to show a slightly better picture than is realistic as the company gets deeper and deeper into the mire.

Go back to the list of four easily identifiable signposts that was given in the last chapter. Study the information presented in the management accounts of your business and try to decide which of the problems besetting you is best described by one of those four. Has turnover been falling? Have margins been declining? Have lead times been lengthening? Have creditor days extended?

Because of their inter-relatedness it is unlikely that you are going to find that there is any single reason that can be isolated – they will all be displayed to some extent. But try to home in on the major cause. And once you have done that begin to ask yourself the question 'Why?', going through all the ramifications until you can get no further.

If you have luck on your side then the reason might be glaringly obvious from the information that you can easily harvest: perhaps a major contract missed; a particular job which took too long against the budgeted time; a bad estimating error; over-optimistic forecasting of market size or the rate at which orders were likely to come in.

But few problems in business are ones of single causation. It is more likely that an initial problem has been compounded by an overlay of subsequent problems as managers sought consciously or unconsciously to adapt to a worsening situation by altering activities in reaction to what they perceived – wrongly as it happens – as completely new problems instead of an outgrowth of an old one. By definition, these adjustments must have been wrong, since if they had been successful, the company would not have arrived at its present problems.

Whatever the reason – or more likely *reasons*, then – they should be identified and understood as completely as possible.

Where the reason for the problem is not immediately obvious, managers who have been intimately involved with the direction of a company to this point – where the examination is taking place – need to review the information that is available to them dispassionately to see if they missed something that was not apparent at the time. It is usually possible to achieve some sort of objective view about when the first *symptoms* of a problem became apparent even if that does not coincide with the *birth* of the problem.

While it is unlikely that the reason for a company's problems will be completely obscure, it is very likely that different members of the management will have different explanations for the causes. These differing theories need to be resolved between managers, and a common explanation or set of explanations agreed upon if progress is to be made in getting out of the difficulty or difficulties – whatever they may be. In simple terms, if the managers cannot agree on what brought them to their current position and find the landmark that they need, then they are still temporarily uncertain and have not broken one of the components of being lost; they have not started the process which will lead to a solution.

This process of coming to a unanimous conclusion about what caused the problems can be very hard and (apparently) damaging organisationally. Established positions may have to discarded; reputations may take a knock. Working relationships may be strained as weaknesses are shown up. The basis on which a business has been run may be shown to be erroneous and some managers may feel badly threatened. Unfortunately for the individual managers concerned, this period may be one that exposes weaknesses of judgement or practice that cannot be tolerated if the company is to pull through.

Overriding everything, though, is the need to complete the analysis speedily. It is likely that the need for doing the job quickly will result in it being done slightly roughly. There is usually little time to be wasted in soothing bruised egos while trying to sort out the company's problems – although you have to remember that damage done now may cause problems later as the recovery gets under way, either because of damaged confidence or because of a well-nursed hostility from a perceived snub or rebuke. But the basic rule is, better a bruised ego than a pristine P45.

The other way in which the process can be damaging, though, is that it may take a lot of time to resolve exactly what is the basic weakness of organisation or operation that has led to the current set of problems. Time spent in studying yesterday's problems is time that is taken away, inevitably, from managing today's. While it is important to get to the roots of the problem if possible, a sensible balance has to be struck between the need for analysis and the onset of paralysis. Perhaps the quickest and cleanest way of arriving at the information you need is to conduct a SWOT analysis.

By forming a small team of senior staff to analyse the Strengths and Weaknesses of the organisation and the Opportunities and Threats that face it, an agenda for rectification of the problems that face the company can be quickly built up which can command the support of all the managers. An example of a SWOT analysis from a real company is given in Case Study 1 at the end of the book, and we shall return to the technique in greater detail in Chapter 4.

However, you should always remember that spending a long time on analysing past problems means that you are probably spending insufficient time on dealing with new problems as they arise. This is likely to get you into deeper trouble. It is also a breach of the cardinal rule of recovery. Remember the aviation principle: Aviate; Navigate; Communicate. The primary task of the manager is to keep the business going just as the pilot's principal duty is to keep the aircraft flying.

The dangers of becoming overly concerned with finding the absolute root of the problem at the expense of dealing with the fresh everyday problems that will also overwhelm the business is particularly acute if the problem is not one is that is immediately obvious – a subtle problem, by definition, is one that takes a lot longer to detect – so that it can do more damage before it is resolved.

So, as we have said, the first stage of the recovery is to take stock of where you are by seeing how you got there. This is the kernel of the whole recovery process. You have to find the nature of the problems that have brought you low before you can begin to tackle them and the best way to start might be the process that we have identified above. If you lash out blindly at what you think may be the problem, you may be striking at the wrong thing.

So where should you look to find the problems? Is there a process for finding out what went wrong? The answer is that, apart from the SWOT analysis already mentioned (and to which we shall return), there is . . . sort of.

The potential range of problems is as large as the number of businesses that get into trouble – and as we noted at the outset, the infuriating thing about general advice and case studies is that they never exactly match your own circumstances. But there are some general rules that can be used to help narrow down the range. Looking at these will help to put the nature of the problem in perspective so that you can then go on to take recovery actions. They will also help you to prepare for the SWOT analysis so that you can sort out the true reasons presented to you from the spurious ones.

(1) *Review the simple things first.* Are the accounts and management information up to the task? Is there a failure of simple control somewhere? If you find out that the information that you need to make an assessment just isn't available quickly or in the form that you want it, then you have probably located the root of the problem.

(2) *Look out for anomalies* in the trend given by your management information so that you can sharpen your analysis of one particular area. Does one particular area of the accounting or management information available to you consistently show a result at variance with the other parts? Does all your information point you to a conclusion different from that shown by your bank balance? If it does then investigate that area further and find out why.

(3) *Review previous forecasts* carefully to see if there is a persistent trend of over-optimism in one part of the business. Gearing a business up with stock levels or manpower to cope with a level of trading never achieved is an all-too-frequent cause of decline. Salesmen are by nature optimists or they wouldn't be in the job. Their forecasts have to be proved by outcome before they can be relied upon. (Incidentally, if you are employing a salesman who is not an optimist, you should probably part company. Unfounded optimism is one thing and responsible criticism is another, but no capable salesman should be a Jeremiah on a long-term basis.)

(4) *Consider the actions of your major competitors* – for clues about what they are doing right. Study where they have made sensible strategic decisions and then apply the same principles to your own business.

(5) *Review the efficiency of the business or critical parts of it,* subjectively, without quantification – test your assumptions and then act. It is generally simpler and quicker to act on intuition and then test your conclusions against any objective data you may have to see if your assessments are correct rather than trawl laboriously through all the information in the hope that the answer will come up and bite you. After all, you have to start somewhere so it might as well be where you think the problem lies.

(6) *Extend your analysis to include external factors* – for instance, have your problems been brought about by bank action or customers extending credit terms unilaterally?

(7) *Consult as widely, but as quickly, as you can* – ask the opinions and advice of your workforce if you think that it will help; talk to your auditors and enlist the help of your bank manager if that can be done circumspectly.

(8) *Beware of simplistic solutions* (but see (1) above). Test your conclusions against the opinions of others and always back your judgement with *realistic* assessments of the available data where they exist. If no data exist, do the best you can with first principles argument; but beware of making judgements based on personal prejudice. Don't bend the data to fit the prejudice you first thought of.

(9) *Don't be frightened to accept the conclusions* that your analysis brings you to, even if they are unpalatable for some others – or to you!

The process of breaking down the first of the three components of being lost, in order to establish what needs to be remedied, is something which can be done effectively only by the individuals on the spot. External advice is all very well but it is no substitute for touching and feeling.

But it is important to remember that it is precisely a *process* of breaking down the overall problem into progressively smaller and smaller parts that will help you. The answer may not appear immediately, but through sensible application of the technique of breaking it into manageable pieces the large problem gets smaller and smaller until it can be dealt with by using the information available.

Establishing the Most Probable Area of where you are is the best that you can hope to do. When time presses and there is a need to act fast, don't strive for Complete Information and Absolute Certainty – you are better off with their poor but honest cousins Approximately Right and Very Likely.

Key points

1. The first job is to keep the business going while finding out what went wrong.

2. Unless a current management policy is manifestly wrong, and will bring the business down in days, continue doing what you are doing until you have valid information to warrant a change of direction.

3. Review available management information to see if you can detect when and where things began to go wrong.

4. Use your own judgement as to where to start looking and if necessary act on that judgement if you are reasonably certain, after consultation, that you have drawn the right conclusions from the available evidence.

5. Beware of the effect of neglecting new problems as they arise in the search for the perfect answer to your existing problems.

Chapter 4

Taking stock financially

In the last chapter we began to look at implementing the sequence of actions that would bring about recovery. We established a series of steps that could be applied to help cut the overall problem down to a manageable size in order to cope with the otherwise indigestible, individual problems of managing a business that is drifting at the mercy of events rather than being controlled purposefully.

Over this and the next two chapters we shall examine each of these steps in detail to provide a series of prompts for specific actions. In business terms, we are going to try to take control of events rather than have to react to every change of circumstance. The result of these considerations will be the business plan for recovery. To return to thinking of our business in terms of flying an aeroplane, we are going to implement the advice given to trainee pilots: you are going to get ahead of the aeroplane so that *you* control *it* rather than let *it* control *you*.

The start of the recovery process began with establishing a procedure for thinking about the recovery. By starting the process that way, a number of things happen automatically: you set out the steps for what you have to do; you become aware of the importance of what you have to do – in theoretical terms, at least; and you establish the beginnings of restoring morale in knowing – and communicating – that instead of drifting aimlessly and being battered further off course by each successive mishap, you are initiating actions that will bring about recovery.

But there is a danger in describing the process in this way in that an impression is conveyed of things happening in a gentle sequential order with every problem following on from its predecessor, like a procession of carnival floats. In fact, the problems that are present in recovering a company come to meet you like the runners at the start of a horse race – in a rush, with a great deal of bunching, and getting bigger as they approach.

There will be no time to deal with problems sequentially, one by one. You will have to make rapid assessments about the priorities that you assign to problems and deal with them as you can. The trick is to adopt a *procedure* whereby you can assign priorities to problems as they come at you, so that even if you do not deal with things in exactly the right order revealed by hindsight, then at least you do not allow any one problem to overwhelm you by neglecting it until it is too late to deal with it.

To trespass on the content of the next chapter slightly, you will have to remember, in doing this, that very many of the people that you are dealing with in the company will want to dump their problems on you so that they can avoid the unpleasant responsibility of having to make difficult decisions. Some of the people you are working with will probably look at the situation and say to themselves that if you have put your hand up to lead them out of this set of problems, then – as far as they are concerned – they have the right to abdicate responsibility for making decisions from here on in.

You have to avoid this pernicious tendency at all costs and push problem solving as far down the line as it will go, while establishing rigorously and quickly the guidelines within which people will be allowed to operate. The best way of doing this is to establish very quickly what your financial position is. Once this boundary is marked then you have solved some of the difficulties in setting priorities since problems will fall into a natural ranking – depending on whether their solution can be afforded or not.

But, unfortunately, this is where another facet of the sequential/coincident issue arises. The difficult decisions which will face you in trying to bring the business round will depend for their solution partly on the quality of the information that you can bring to bear on unravelling the problem and partly on the quality of the people that you can use to help you implement the solution. Both of these will probably be suspect in a company in trouble – at least in their totality if not in individual cases.

What this means is that you are going to have to make decisions on the hoof about *how* to deal with problems at the same time as you decide *who* is best equipped to help to solve them and then, furthermore – and very differently – *whom* you can trust to do things effectively and according to your instructions.

To mix the analogies we have been using, the whole business is a bit like the captain of a football team picking the players while the game is in progress rather than before it starts. If you have been associated with the business for a long time, then of course you will have a better idea of the capabilities of the members of your potential team and can adjust your strategy accordingly. If not, you are going to have to make rapid judgements at the same time as being prepared to be very flexible in your attitude and harsh in your assessments. You do not have the luxury of time to give people lots of chances to prove themselves when you are trying to keep a company afloat. At the same time you may find that someone whom you did not rate initially is more than capable of doing a difficult task when provided with the right leadership.

But to return to the central task and central problem, let us also revert to the aviating analogy. Money is the fuel of a business and your aircraft has been flying along, losing height, unable to stem a leak in its tanks. As the pilot of the plane, you want to know two things immediately to help you to determine your strategy and plan your recovery route:

- how long will the fuel that you have left on board last you at the present rate of consumption;
- how can you reduce consumption of fuel to extend the duration of what you have left.

These are two very different classes of problems and require different treatment and a different approach from each other: one is a question of resorting to fact, the other of exercising judgement.

The unfortunate pilot in this situation would probably do two things: tap the fuel gauge to make sure that it was registering correctly, and ask the flight engineer or navigator to make a quick calculation of how much fuel was left. The pilot would then determine how the aeroplane could be trimmed differently to ensure that the best use was made of the fuel available to extend the plane's flying time. The crew members might also be asked if they had any good ideas.

You certainly have to do two of the above actions – checking the availability of cash and asking the accountant to make a forecast of future cashflows – and you may also consider doing the last, by consulting with members of the management, and possibly consulting even wider within the company. But remember, the answer to the first question will be available from looking at the facts – or what will pass for the facts in the situation you find yourself in – while the answer to the second will be very much a matter for your own judgement and leadership.

Stripped of the analogy, the following are stages that you go through in taking stock of your financial position.

(1) *Institute a thorough review of your financial position* to encompass the three elements:

- current bank balance;
- future certain and foreseeable cash demands arranged by time;
- asset position.

All these are to be broken down as finely as possible and are to be available to you within a maximum of forty-eight hours of your initial request.

Setting a tight deadline in this first exercise will have the additional benefit of helping you to assess whether the accountant/ finance director is on top of their task. The way in which the end result is presented to you will also give you a good indication of the quality of the management information available and the robustness of the systems.

If this essentially simple information cannot be made available to you within forty-eight hours then the likelihood is that there is something seriously wrong with the organisation of the accounts department. You should investigate the department as a matter of urgency since a good number of crucial future decisions are going to be based on what information can be supplied by accounts. If this information is late, defective or wrong your decisions will be the same.

(2) *Establish a small team* – probably the finance director (if the first exercise was completed adequately), the sales director and the head of shop-floor operations in addition to yourself – to consider the operational needs of the business and the major failings that it currently suffers from. Establish a simple remit for this group (something along the lines that it can consider any aspect of the business), explain that purpose from the outset and use it as your steering group for all future actions. Make sure that the group meets regularly – at least every day in the first few days, probably at the beginning and the end of each day to review what should be done and what has been done.

The cohesiveness of this group will be a crucial factor in the success of the recovery. The recovery will probably only work if they behave as a united team and have a common purpose. In pursuit of this, it is a sensible first step to have them discuss openly the special circumstances of the situation and encourage themselves by discussion to see that there is a way out. The best way of doing this is to set aside half a morning for a SWOT analysis, looking at the Strengths of the business; its Weaknesses; the Opportunities open to it; and the Threats it faces.

The purpose of this exercise is to produce a list of points that can be followed up with action after being agreed upon by the members of the recovery team. By looking at all the four areas in turn a ready-made agenda for action is developed which will have the implicit agreement of those who brought it into being. Break the problem down into small and easily tackled steps. Once the list has been thought up, priorities should be attached to each of the items on the list – and perhaps some might be accorded a ranking beyond their significance to the immediate recovery because of the perceived importance of making some quick impact on the business.

For instance, it may be better to improve the physical appearance of the staff toilets if this will produce an immediate lift in morale, rather than to concentrate exclusively on long-range goals which produce no visible results for some time. But you must beware giving the impression of merely fiddling while Rome burns.

When the priorities have been established by broad agreement you must begin to initiate action. Make the group members responsible for taking actions in specific areas and ensure that individual responsibilities are well understood. (This will be covered in greater detail in the next chapter.)

(3) *Review the outgoings* that you have established from the first exercise: all payments to creditors, statutory bodies, for imminent and forthcoming materials and supplies demanded by the business and, not least, the emoluments of all personnel. Make a list of them all and then proceed down that list thinking about each payment as if you had to meet it personally. Freeze or defer every single payment that you can and come down particularly hard on any superfluous expenditure – conferences that can be cancelled (even if it involves accepting a modest cash penalty), planned staff parties, excessive entertaining or unnecessary foreign visits, even bonus payments that can be deferred, are all good candidates for the chop.

You must steel yourself to reject every plea for special treatment for this particular case and that particular example unless you are absolutely convinced that the argument in favour of retaining the expense is overwhelming. Your sole preoccupation must be sheltering and preserving your cash resources. You can always release money later but it is impossible to recover money that has already been spent.

Similarly, don't get dragged into spending more money just because you have already spent a modest amount on doing something. That money has gone. The balance notionally allocated for the remainder of the expenditure can be saved and devoted to a more purposeful use if required.

(4) Next , *have revised cashflows produced*, within a maximum of a week of the first financial snapshot exercise (which detailed only cash resources, outgoings and assets). The cashflows will incorporate incoming revenue as well as outgoings – but based on the most pessimistic yet still realistic basis available – so that you know the worst case that you face. Marry these up with the forecast of cash demands that you first established to ensure that they are consistent and then begin to feed these to your small working group so that they can make adjustments to the operation of the business – either positive or negative – to keep within the available cash resources.

(5) Within a week of starting, *look very carefully at selling assets* that are not essential to the running of the business. Look at (a) property, (b) cars and (c) surplus stock.

(a) **Property**
In general terms, it is unnecessary for almost any business to own the property it occupies. Selling a freehold – even if the property market is soggy – can produce cash that can provide the way out of the crisis. Renting is usually cheaper and more flexible, for virtually every type of business. The business of the business that you are in is the manufacture of widgets or gold bricks or whatever. Unless you are dealing with a property company, it is *not* the owning of property.

If the business that you are concerned with has an overdraft and that overdraft is resistant to every effort to reduce it through trading, then think of the cause of that borrowing (which is the company's Achilles' heel) as being the property which the business owns – because it almost certainly is. Money currently locked in bricks and mortar could have been used to provide for current cash. If you had that cash, there might not be any crisis.

You can make use of the errors of your predecessors, though, by turning a potential millstone into your salvation. Don't delay; *do it*.

In addition, look very carefully at any form of split-site operation. There isn't a formal law, as far as I know, that states specifically that problems grow as the square of the distance between two sites – but there ought to be. Multiple separate sites mean problems of control, accounting and communication. Running a business from more than one site also gives people a chance to hide – and more than one weak manager has been known to use the possibilities of being at the wrong site at the right time in split-site operations to avoid confronting problems head-on.

Split sites will almost certainly mean duplication of some resources and therefore of cost. It is certain to mean that your effort is diluted while you shuttle between locations, however closely located they might be. Obviously a few types of operation do require that there be more than one site for the business to be run effectively but, generally speaking, one site is best if the business can be arranged that way.

(b) **Cars**
One of the easiest ways of releasing money quickly for a business in trouble is to take a radical review of car policy. Most businesses can easily relinquish chunks of their car fleet without any serious damage to the efficacy of operation. At the very least, some of the expensive machinery sitting in the car park can be replaced with cheaper, more economical models (with the double benefit that cash is immediately released and running costs are reduced for the future).

If it can't be done – or if spurious reasons are presented as to why it can't be done – then you have a good clue to the values of the management. A manager who values a car more than the job – and demonstrates it by being difficult over company car policy in a time of crisis – or a fleet manager who made an original deal that can't be backed out of or modified for changes of circumstances – is probably not a manager that you will want to keep for the long term.

But beware here, too. While company car policies generate the most ridiculous attitudes among otherwise sensible people who should know better, you may make a serious mistake if you push too hard for unsuitable changes. It is no good reducing the vehicle expenses of a sales team by 10 per cent if by so doing you reduce their selling capacity by 40 per cent because they are using unsuitable vehicles under your new regime.

(c) **Surplus stock**
The sale of surplus stock and equipment can provide a useful route for raising modest amounts of cash as well as making better use of available space and improving manufacturing discipline. Don't neglect looking at what may appear to be small-scale savings. Clearing out redundant but still serviceable stock or equipment can lead you to further substantial savings in store costs, accommodation and manufacturing as space is liberated and stocking practices are purged.

(6) *Beware of skipping wage payments. In extremis,* when cash is not immediately available but is *certain* to be available within *a matter of hours* then it may be permissible to ask employees if they would defer taking their wages and salaries so that you do not breach covenants or cash limits. But be very careful about missing weekly or monthly basic payments to employees.

There are two main reasons for this, one practical and one ethical. In practical terms you may find that all you have done by missing a monthly or weekly payment is to make the following one more of a problem. It may seem like a good idea at the time to try to save money temporarily, but skipping a payment will only cause further problems with morale and double the pressure next time a payment is due, if the previous one has not been paid off. In times like those you are facing, the last thing you need is a disaffected workforce.

Perhaps more weightily, in ethical terms it is fundamentally unfair to ask employees to take the risks that shareholders ought to be taking, without any of the rewards that shareholders can expect.

Remember too, that while there might be a rough justice in asking people to do without pay in the short term in order to retain their jobs, you run other risks by deferring wages. First, it is generally better for all concerned that people should worry about the execution of the tasks of their job than about how they are going to meet the next mortgage payment. Second, by cutting wages you run the risk of losing your best people – those whose efforts will contribute to the recovery of the company – and not just those that you can do without. Third, news of such actions travels like wildfire and may have the effect of further destabilising your creditors, to your detriment.

Asking people to forego bonuses which can be deferred – one of the first actions that you should have considered – is a very different thing from asking them to forego wages and salaries. While there are still elements of both the practical and the ethical objections in doing this – for the purist – they are less pronounced, more arguable and will certainly have less serious repercussions on the future cashflow of the business.

(7) *Document what you do as you go along* so that you can incorporate the changes that you make in the next stage of your recovery plan.

(8) *Let the bank know what you are doing as quickly as possible* so that they are aware that something positive is happening. Unless the situation has got to a stage where the bank has no option left but to close you down by calling in its loans – in which case you are wasting your time, anyway – it will probably allow you more time so long as it is evident that positive actions are being taken to try to recover the situation. (Dealing with the bank is given its own chapter later on, when the full range of considerations is discussed, but the point bears repetition.)

(9) *Take care that you are still trading legally.* There is a fine difference between trading insolvently and trading fraudulently. Trading insolvently implies that the company cannot meet its obligations as they fall due but might be able to meet them otherwise in the course of trading, while trading fraudulently means that the company can never meet its obligations. The latter is illegal and carries serious criminal penalties (see Appendix 4).

Essentially, if it is your opinion after having studied all the facts at your disposal, and to the best of your knowledge and belief, that you can improve your creditors' position by remaining in business, then you may be entitled to continue to trade. You should be prepared to justify your belief factually in a court of law if need be. Take care also that your fellow directors are aware of the situation and agree with your evaluation. To be seen to have reached this decision absolutely correctly, you should consider the options only after you have taken specialist advice. Above all, for your own protection if the worst comes to the worst, you should maintain careful records of the meetings held to consider the matter of whether or not you are entitled to continue to trade.

Your auditors may not be the best people to ask about the legality of your position, since they may well be as much concerned about their own skins as yours. Remember, auditors are employed to check the books for statutory purposes; they are not employed, as auditors, to take business decisions. You will do better to ask an insolvency practitioner to advise you if you are seriously concerned about the circumstances of trading. Most large accounting firms will have a practitioner or a specialist department prepared to offer informal advice, usually free of charge for an initial consultation.

Key points

1. Make a quick and rough assessment of the financial position of the company to determine how much cash and assets you have that you can draw on.

2. Husband your cash – reduce all unnecessary expenditure, eliminate waste and think carefully about the cash implications of the organisation of your business.

3. Create a small group of managers who will meet regularly to review all aspects of the business and undertake actions for change.

4. Start to build a preliminary recovery plan based on the information you have begun to gather; avoid any assumption of increased sales. Talk to the bank about your plans.

5. Sell off assets not absolutely essential, to prolong the availability of your cash.

6. Have the management team conduct a SWOT analysis of the business – but only after you have begun to take actions to prolong the cash availability.

7. Beware analysis paralysis.

Chapter 5

Taking stock managerially

Building and running a business satisfactorily is about combining three elements into a workable blend: money, opportunity and people. If opportunity falters then the company can possibly jog along for a little while until things pick up again or until astute managers perceive a new opportunity in a different area. If money fails, then the situation is quite clear. The company either has to be folded or more money has to be squeezed out of somewhere – operations, the product, or the pockets of shareholders – to keep it going. But while the absence of sufficient money is usually the major apparent cause that precipitates an acute crisis in a business, it may very effectively obscure deeper problems that stem from the poor management of people.

The implication of this is that the best plans for recovery, on paper, will come to nothing in reality if they are not followed through successfully by people who understand what they are doing and why they are doing it, and have the determination and the energy to bring about the success of what has been planned. For this to be done, the management resources of the business have to equal – or be made equal to – the strain thrown upon the business.

In other words, if people's activities – *at all levels throughout the company* – are not managed properly, a recovery is an almost impossible achievement. If the plan for recovery is going to succeed, then, it is obviously of paramount importance that the turnround manager takes stock very quickly of the capacities and abilities of colleagues throughout the business, so that three things can be done:

1. use can be made of what is available;
2. allowances can be made for what is not available;
3. a start can be made on adapting the existing managerial style *throughout the business* to what is desirable or necessary.

So part of this chapter will be concerned with determining the strengths and weaknesses of an existing management team and making it effectively mesh with the plan for recovery. Part will be concerned with the changes that have to be considered in establishing a new and better management style – perhaps more properly defined as instilling a new management culture in the business.

Businesses often fail – usually fail – because of some shortcoming in the way they are run, rather than because of any single catastrophic event. This can be distilled into a shorthand that the managerial culture is not adequate for the task involved. In taking over from the previous managers in an effort to reverse a long-standing decline, it will be the underlying task of the turnround manager to instil a new managerial culture into the business so that the circumstances which brought about the decline do not recur. Recovering a business from the brink only to have it fall again because the recovery is not well founded is like catching a falling plate only to drop it again: the relief at saving it is very temporary and the outcome is the same, only more effort has been wasted.

This new culture has to replace the shortcomings of the way that the business was managed previously and build upon the particular characteristics of the business so that it is tailored for the circumstances the company faces. Regrettably for those who seek simple solutions, there can be no ideal model of a management culture that can be slipped into every situation and will work regardless, since it is an intangible thing; but aspects of it, and general principles, can be identified so that a framework can be produced and applied satisfactorily.

From experience, most people in small companies work best in an environment where their individual contribution to the progress of the business is conspicuous and can be identified. Accepting responsibility is not a problem for most people provided that they are not pushed beyond their own capacities or asked to bear the risk of undue penalties which they have no opportunity to avoid by their own efforts.

But for this to happen, individual employees will have to be bolstered by a management style at the top of the business which reinforces their own efforts. This means that the managers have to instil in the organisation a culture that encourages and fosters the following:

- attention to detail, so that needless duplication of time and effort is eliminated; this has become known as the 'right first time' principle;
- the encouragement of risk-taking within established limits, now often wrongly referred to by the unthinking application of the fashionable rubric of 'empowerment';
- the maximum use of abilities within the company at all levels;
- effective communication of the purpose of the company to all engaged in it;

- elimination of needless hierarchy – since hierarchy, carried beyond the necessary requirements of establishing responsibility, is a pernicious device built up by those unable to do their own jobs properly and therefore anxious to hide their own inadequacies behind rule books.

The installation of this culture inside a business requires – often – the dismantling of what is already there in favour of a newer, looser structure. There are many aspects to this, of course, and the circumstances will differ from company to company depending on the individual culture of each. Absolute prescriptions are of limited value as a result. However, it is possible to prescribe that if you are going to change a culture you can choose to do it in one of two ways: you can adopt the gradualist approach and change things around the margin – or you can be radical and go for the throat.

Obviously, both of these methods have arguments in their favour and carry their own particular drawbacks. Horses have to be chosen for courses but it may be wise to bear in mind the following:

1. A wholesale elimination of a management structure will bring about considerable learning requirements for the managers brought in to replace the lost structure. This will probably retard the recovery process, unless the incomers are particularly talented or know the business well through some other means; equally it might be argued that to replace a set of (collectively) failed managers is the only way to ensure the success of any new plans.
2. Bringing in outsiders may well enable fresh eyes to view the business's problems but may also provoke adverse reactions among junior staff who see their own pathways to promotion now blocked by younger, fresher incumbents.
3. Outsiders, depending on their point of view, may take comfort from seeing the inefficient old guard eliminated from the business or may find it hard to understand what is going on from their particular vantage point and treat any changes with caution.

As with most management problems there is probably no one clear answer: a combination of removal and replacement by outsiders, and internal reshuffling and promotion from within is likely to provide the safest route to solving the managerial problem. Management teams are rarely completely dud and the benefit of experience (of the way that a business operates on a medium-term basis) is a valuable asset too frequently discarded – as the UK clearing banks are now learning after the middle management purges of the late 1980s and early 1990s.

However, there is one particular problem very common in businesses in trouble which must be eliminated very quickly. It is all too usual in a business that is experiencing problems to find that everyone tries to do everybody else's job – to the detriment of all of the jobs that need to be done. It is a problem that requires swift treatment if it is not to threaten the continued existence of the business.

Trying to do someone else's job in addition to your own is a natural reaction to seeing colleagues under pressure; it comes partly from a desire to pitch in during times of difficulty and is also partly down to the individual's belief that they can probably do the job better than the incumbent.

Sales directors believe in their heart of hearts that they could do the managing director's job better than the person who has got it (and who doesn't understand customers); finance directors know that they could do the sales director's job better than the sales director (if only they were allowed to exercise some basic financial discipline over the sales force); managing directors *know* that they can do a better job than anyone else because they are *managing* directors, after all.

When this problem arises and is allowed to persist, it is symptomatic of a deep malaise in the business – effectively a complete disregard for suitable and effective operational management. For no matter what anyone involved in interfering might think they are doing, the fact of the matter is that they are probably making things worse. People are employed to do *specific jobs* not to dabble in someone else's province. If the finance director is not up to the job then that person should go and be replaced by someone who is; if the works director is a lousy organiser who cannot control production adequately, then that person should make way for someone who can. Concealing a colleague's chronic failings by covering up and helping out is being an accessory after the fact.

Doing somebody else's job instead of your own may also be a mechanism of escape from the overbearing responsibilities of a job that has become too tough to complete in times of great difficulty. It is, for instance, no fun coming into work each day to work in an accounts department knowing that you are going to have to deal with a crop of phone calls from irate suppliers who are thirty, forty or fifty days overdue in receiving their payments. It is much easier and less stressful to occupy your time diligently compiling sales statistics for the sales director or dealing with the errors in the assets register.

Nor is it any fun if you are a supervisor in charge of a section trying to build a machine for a customer who wants it to a deadline after which there are penalty clauses, if the parts you need are in continually short supply because you are on stop with a number of suppliers – because the overloaded accounts clerk will not speak to them to tell them when they might expect payment. After a while it becomes far easier and personally more productive to set the stores system to rights or to update the health and safety policy for your section.

At junior operational levels, interference in the jobs of others is an irritation which can lead to costly mistakes and might get worse – but it is a situation that is usually sorted out by the simple requirements of the tasks involved: usually only one person can turn a screwdriver, operate a lathe, fill in a customer report form. Generally speaking, problems of this sort at this level are not immediately life-threatening as far as the business is concerned, provided they are not chronic.

At the administrative level, though, the situation is markedly worse since the scope for duplication and error is that much expanded by the nature of the tasks. Territories are less well-defined operationally, both because of the tasks themselves and because of the occasional need for transferability between tasks so that holiday and sickness cover operates successfully. Jobs left undone at this level because individuals are trying to take on someone else's role can have serious consequences that may take a long time to unravel.

At the managerial level the situation is very different again. Mistakes here can have catastrophic effects within a relatively short space of time since the efforts of so many others can be misdirected by the failure of one person to carry out their own responsibilities effectively or because they have confused a simple situation that would be under control if it were in the hands of one person.

This is not an easy challenge. Unless you are very perceptive – or you have been involved with the business for a long time – it is not easy to make a correct, *quick* judgement about how well individuals are acquitting themselves in their jobs. Quick judgements about how well someone is doing are easy – but may not be correct. Someone may be doing a very good job in such difficult circumstances that the results do not reflect the effort involved. But if that particular person were not in that job the results might be very much worse. If you make a judgement that because the job is not showing the results that you expect, the wrong person is doing it, you might compound the problem.

But it is slightly easier to make *reasonably* accurate judgements about how well a specific job is being done. That should be the starting point for any analysis. There are five basic steps in doing this piece of analysis:

1. *examine* the business dispassionately to try to find the pressure points in the operation;
2. *organise* your own views about how effectively those pressure points are being dealt with;
3. *consult* with your colleagues in general terms – not in detailed personal terms – about their appreciation of where the pressure points are and how they are dealt with;

4. *review* your own opinions in the light of the discussions;
5. *act* on your conclusions to eliminate the problems.

There cannot be two people setting the course for recovery whose views and opinions will conflict with each other. So *you* have to make sure that there is only one person doing any of the jobs that need to be done, which means that you have to sort out the priorities for individual jobs – your view must prevail.

The least abrasive way of doing this is to institute a job description scheme, at the earliest opportunity, so that everyone knows what they are doing: what they should be doing and equally what they should *not* be doing. This simple management tool is an invaluable means of assisting you in putting together your team for maximum effect. How can someone do their job properly unless they know what they are supposed to be doing? And how can you evaluate them unless you know what you are measuring them against?

Assuming there is a system already in place, then utilise it as a ready-made bench-mark against which to evaluate individuals (but make sure that the job description against which you are going to evaluate them is up-to-date and accurately describes their tasks at the moment). The first of these evaluations might be after the recovery has been under way for a month and another made again at three months.

Take the performance of your senior managers over the first month, match it against the job description that they have set against their titles, heading by heading, and see how well they have performed, making notes about their performance as you do. This is probably best done informally after so brief a period, with the conclusions that you reach being part of the preparation for a formal review after three months. Despite the informality of the one-month exercise there is purpose to the note-taking about the performance of individuals over the initial evaluation period: in the welter of things that will happen in the first three months it is very easy both to forget salient points about individual performance and to overlook individuals' contributions. By preparing brief notes for your own purposes you can see if there has been any improvement or deterioration between the first and subsequent evaluations in a methodical fashion. (The point about note-taking has already been touched on in Chapter 1.)

You should encourage your managers to do the same for their staff too, so that everyone knows that there is a process of continuous evaluation being carried on. If there is no system ask the senior managers to institute one very soon after you begin to devise your own plan, both as a method of checking on the assumptions in your own plan and as a method of making sure that all the areas that you will have outlined in your SWOT analysis are properly covered by appropriate managers with appropriate responsibilities.

The need for there to be only one pilot in charge of the aeroplane has already been emphasised at the earliest point of this book. But it bears repetition and a small case study may help to illuminate the point that there are more ways of skinning the cat than simply the most direct approach.

The managing director and chairman of a company which I was involved with for quite some time spent long hours out of the office on 'business' as a method of avoiding the unpleasant decisions that had to be taken to get his company – of which he was the sole shareholder – out of the mire. This 'business' involved meeting potential clients (who never delivered orders), conferring with advisers (whose expensive advice he never applied) and travelling to exhibitions and trade shows to keep up to date with the opposition (from whose experiences he never learned). When he was in the factory he interfered with the responsibilities of others, countermanded their valid instructions and set people to work on his own pet projects – which often disrupted urgent production schedules.

Because of the fact that he was chairman, managing director and sole shareholder, he was effectively an immovable object in terms of the business's organization. He was also a very costly component of the company's overheads. His lack of contribution was resented by his colleagues. There was a distinct school of thought when the business hit the rocks in terms of cashflow that he should stop wasting time and money and bring his many talents firmly inside the business. For a time he was engaged in the recovery but his short attention span and the attractions of competing diversions rapidly lured him back to his old ways.

In fact, looked at more dispassionately, his absences gave the others who were more focussed than he the opportunity to get things done that would have taken much longer to do with his active involvement. Effectively, in a time of crisis, because of these failings, he was better occupied out of the business than in it. Once this was perceived, the others spent less time carping about the MD's behaviour and more in attending to the recovery, and less time in trying to double up on tasks in case someone had been diverted by a special instruction resulting from one of the MD's whims. (That company survived because of a lot of hard work on the part of others, because its products were essentially very good and because, as an individual, the chairman/managing director was blessed with good luck – which, as we shall see in another chapter, is a prerequisite for recovery.)

But ordinarily, whatever the reason for the situation, whatever the level involved, the outcomes of duplication of job execution will be the same: confusion and overlap; mistakes and uncertainty. Even if things eventually work out for the good, much effort can be expended unnecessarily in sorting out problems that a good system, robustly adhered to, would not have permitted to arise in the first place. And inevitably, during the time it takes to sort things out, the situation will be deteriorating rather than improving, as crucial but difficult jobs are left undone while easier and unimportant tasks occupy the attention of everyone.

Sorting out the tangle of responsibilities is not an easy task and is made more complicated by the reluctance of individuals to let go of what they have accumulated in management responsibility terms. A reasonably quick and clean way of tackling the problem is to install, very rapidly, individual responsibility among senior managers for portions of the recovery budget. By making managers individually responsible for turnover (which they will like) and costs (which they will not) it is usually possible in one or two meetings to establish effective lines of managerial control reasonably quickly. This process of saddling managers with responsibility has a number of further and very obvious benefits in controlling the recovery process. Crucially, it indicates areas of managerial weakness quickly; it forces managers to get to know their areas of operation intimately if they are not to be embarrassed in board meetings; and it enables rapid delegation of the process of control and recovery.

A reinforcement to this is the installation throughout the business of the 'internal customer concept'. Everyone is well aware of the hackneyed cliché that businesses cannot survive without customers. The problem for most businesses is that most employees never come into contact with a customer and so they can take little regard of the distant problems that the failure to supply on time to budget and to specification can produce. But what everyone has experience of is *being* a customer – in a baker's shop; in a furniture showroom; of the electricity company; of a local builder; of a bank. So the internal customer concept effectively says that everyone inside the business should forget about The Customer – unless they have direct contact with that mythical entity – and should instead regard the person with whom they next deal *inside the business* as being *their own* customer. Equally, everyone inside the business is a customer of the others with whom they come into contact. Since very few people are willing to suffer consistently poor service from people with whom they deal in a business relationship, promoting the interest of the internal customer can have a rapid effect on smartening up internal processes and eliminating sloppiness in a business that is in trouble – provided that it is backed up by strong, swift and effective management action.

This commitment to act on the part of the management has to be there to ensure that necessary changes are made. If it is there, then the concept also has the beneficial effect of rapidly improving self-esteem inside the business. Employees suddenly realise that they have the power to force things to be changed that have previously been carried out poorly and to the detriment of all. The internal customer is the other side – and the more effective one, to my mind – of the 'empowerment' coin that is so popular among freely structured companies. Without that effective management support for the concept then embitterment instead of empowerment is likely to be the consequence.

Key points

1. You are going to have to change the management culture in the business if the recovery is going to work effectively.

2. Eliminate very fast and forcefully any tendency on the part of managers to dabble part-time in an area outside their individual competence.

3. Install a job description system so that everyone's respective responsibilities are fully documented both for their own purposes and for the purposes of future monitoring.

4. You must move to a culture where maximum freedom is allowed to responsible individuals and where everyone fully understands their respective responsibilities and all areas of business management are adequately covered.

5. To help you do this, push budgetary responsibility as far down the organisation as you think it can be successfully operated.

6. The culture you are trying to encourage effectively says forget The Customer. That person doesn't exist for most people in the business. For most employees the true customer is the next person *inside the business* with whom they deal.

Chapter 6

Taking stock of the market-place

Once you have looked at the basic resources available to you as a turnround manager – the finance available and the quality of the management team you have at your disposal – you must take stock of the external factors. The single most important of these is what is happening in the market-place that the business operates in.

Changes in the fortunes of a business as a consequence of changes in the market-place can never be entirely separated from the managerial or financial aspects of the problem of decline. One definition of a good manager would be a manager who anticipates or responds very quickly to changes in the market-place in order never to be wrong-footed by market developments. If you are involved with a business that has gone wrong then the chances are that you are also involved with a set of managers who have misread or ignored the signals that the market has given them. You should reorganise the business structure or systems to eliminate the possibility of that happening more than once.

If the same mistakes are not to be made again then an accurate appreciation of what is happening in the market-place must be available to condition the content of the strategy for recovery which you are about to embark upon. It is important for the turnround manager to know what the market the company is trying to sell into looks like since unless you have a good understanding of the factors that affect your product – how, why and when it sells and to whom and at what price – then you could find yourself making very grave errors in writing your recovery plan. To take a couple of absurd examples, the market for fuel logs is limited in summertime; the market for electric cooling fans almost disappears in winter. The author of a recovery plan that predicted increased sales of logs during the summer for a depressed log business or a rapid surge in sales of fans during November and December for a fan maker might well be disappointed in the level of acceptance that it received from a nervous banker.

The shape of the market-place will hold evidence about the factors that have to be taken into account in writing a plan for recovery. Remember that as the turnround manager you are going to be concerned principally with generating cash for the business since what a failing business requires above all else is a boost of cash to give it the breathing space to recover and regroup. Factors such as cyclicality, the degree of competition, the size and number of competitors, the expected level of margin, selling costs and price sensitivity of both customers and product specification will all have a bearing on the rate of flow of cash that can be expected from the sale of products. This will obviously affect the speed of recovery and must be allowed for in the construction of the recovery plan.

Once again we come back to the problem of trying to gather and assimilate a lot of information under difficult circumstances. Ideally, the business should contain much of the data from which the information required can be developed – especially if the business is involved in manufacturing goods. But as we are already aware, well-documented, well-ordered businesses often start to go to pieces under the pressure of financial decline and you cannot rely on receiving the information about the market-place set out like the shelves of a business library. While there may be records of previous sales forecasts or competitor analyses, you may have to consult widely throughout the business to establish which is the major competitor, what products sell best and to whom, and why a certain product consistently lags behind its anticipated sales.

Remember, though, two factors: a mediocre product in the hands of a good salesperson will outsell a good product in the hands of a mediocre salesperson so the reason for poor performance may be linked to personnel considerations rather than price or market factors; and the market's verdict on a product is often final. Few products get a second chance to sell well if the first chance is muffed.You will have to weigh up all the considerations available to you before you reach any conclusions – and, as always, you will be dealing with conditions of uncertainty and partial information.

Certain information should be readily available. The size and impor-tance of competitors should be well known to the incumbent managers and sales staff as should the cyclicality or seasonality of sales. It may be less easy to estimate industry margins or price sensitivity, but an examination of competitors' accounts and information gleaned from reports from the sales force should give a rough and ready indication.

Perhaps most important of all, though, is the sales history of the business you are dealing with. This is not to do with the third-hand information available from the accounts of other companies but with what actually happened to the sales performance of the business that you are seeking to recover. It should give you details of the crucial numbers you will need to found your own appreciation of the market-place that your business deals in, so that you can build up your recovery plan on tailored information: product actually sold during specific periods, both in absolute terms and against forecasts; the details of changing margins; frequency of sales and seasonality of sales. In addition, it is likely to be more up-to-date than anything that you can derive from any other source and so of more immediate use to you.

In this respect, you should treat information about markets from official sources – Business Monitors and DTI statistics – with extreme caution. While they have their uses they are usually very much out-of-date and are compiled at source by people – other business managers – whose interest is in getting them out of the way as quickly as possible rather than in statistical exactitude.

But this sort of information will give you a base from which to appreciate the generalities of the market-place, and once you have established the basic shape of the market-place using the information which you have available to you, you should begin to widen the scope of your analysis to include the particular activities of your major competitors. Analyse what they appear to have done right or wrong so that you can either emulate them or avoid the same mistakes. Although the analysis does not have to be formal, one way of doing this is to get hold of their accounts and perform some simple ratio analysis so that you can compare their activities with your own. In addition to your own edification, bankers on the receiving end of your recovery plan will probably appreciate some indication that you have looked at the competition in arriving at your conclusions. But bear in mind that the object of the exercise is recovering a business not preparing a superlative business plan that covers every aspect of reviving a dead company – dead because the preparation of the business plan took too long!

Since accounts are usually substantially out-of-date by the time that you get them (they are after all matters of historical record) and since ratio analysis is really only worthwhile when you can compare a run of numbers rather than an isolated set, and not least since accounts can conceal as much as they reveal, you might, however, find it more productive just to talk to your salesmen about what the competition does that seems to them to be better than what you do as a business.

As an extension of this process, get hold of some of the products of your major competitors – or at least the product specification – and look at them in comparison with your products as if you were an objective customer. Repeat the process with your senior managers and then get your best salesperson to try to sell the competition's product to you. Try to assess objectively which of the competing products you would buy if you were making the choice, taking account of as many of the facets of the sale as you can consider: design, packaging, literature, sales technique. If the product is a major item of expenditure, consider the differences (if any) in the methods that are employed by your business and by your competitors in financing the sale.

This series of exercises should be completed as quickly as possible: extended analysis is not required; fine detail is not necessary. The completion of the run of analyses is the background to your intended actions not the conclusion of them and the most important part of the process is the creation of a recovery strategy not the intellectualising that accompanies it.

You may find that everything that can be done has been done, in which case you should consider very carefully whether it is practical to continue to try to rescue the business and whether the interests of all concerned would not be better served by an orderly shut-down. There is, after all, only so much that can be done – some planes have to crash-land and the skill of the pilot is then exercised in making the contact with the ground as gentle as possible.

If this is not the case, though, you have to devise a plan to get you back on course. You are still aviating if you have got this far – now you have got to think about navigating.

In Chapter 4 the analogy was drawn with the problem the pilot faced: flying an aircraft that was losing fuel, the pilot's urgent task was to try to extend its range in order to get to the chosen destination. One of the ways of doing that is to reduce the load that the wings have to lift and the engines have to pull by jettisoning some of the excess weight that the plane is carrying. (We shall return to this course of action later in the context of the number of people that the business employs – recovering a business is all about carrying freight and not passengers.)

But for now, jettisoning excess baggage means considering just what it is that your business does. Consider very carefully the purpose for which your business is in business. In Chapter 4 we also argued that most businesses should not own property and that getting rid of freehold or long leasehold property in favour of renting might provide a cash boost. Apply the same logic and think about what you offer the customer. It could be that your product range or service offerings are too numerous. Your customers may believe that you are too widely spread in your abilities and not sufficiently focussed, for instance. Your salespeople may have difficulty in completing sales because they have too much to talk about to be regarded as expert in any one field.

You may be missing customers' business because you have no defined perception yourself of what the business is that you are in. In one business of my acquaintance, it was possible to think of the company as either a medical products company, or a furnishing business or an upholstery company. An accepted definition of which it was, by discussion among the managers as part of the SWOT analysis, helped greatly to focus the company's efforts and had a beneficial effect on the way that the sales force was able to promote the company. By concentrating on one definition, the company's image in the market-place became clearer and the way ahead more sharply delineated.

Over time a business's initial purpose may become obscured. New activities are added to the basic purpose like an oyster covering a piece of grit with successive layers of mother-of-pearl. The covering makes life easier and more comfortable for the oyster; but in a business it often has the effect of slowing down responsiveness and choking agility. Many businesses have grown up in a haphazard fashion, adding bits here and there according to the fancy of the owner or as fashion, expediency or opportunism dictated. These can often be dispensed with at no cost to the effective running of the central operation, so consider disposing of or closing those activities which are not central to the main business; they may even be a source of extra cash.

Of course, some businesses may suffer from the opposite condition: they may be blinkered as opposed to focussed. In contrast to being too widely spread, they may not be doing enough to satisfy their customers' requirements. As before, the analysis of the primary purpose of your business and then considering whether it performs that purpose adequately in the context of proven sales will throw up the answer.

The problem with discovering this route is that it usually leads to a requirement for cash to fund an expansion of activity and the last thing you need is to find that further cash is necessary to expand the business when you already have enough on your plate meeting the day-to-day requirements of working capital. But if you do conclude that you need to expand in order to survive, don't shrink from that conclusion – it gives you the objective towards which you must work. Nor should you shy away from a conclusion that suggests that you should build upon the so-called 'organic strengths' of the business which you are trying to bring back (in other words, the strengths of the business considered as a whole, naturally extending and growing into related areas) in order to survive. Some businesses may be sensibly organised only if they have a supportive structure of a number of activities – dry-cleaning businesses require pressing facilities for instance; garden centres usually have to have a spread of retailing activities to make them viable.

In your deliberations about a route out of your situation, mentally strip back the business to its real purpose. In the light of that, consider what you actually do – the functions that your business actually performs – and evaluate what the business has functionally against what its purpose is. This process has become fashionably known as writing a 'mission statement' for the business. The original term stemmed from space exploration where it was a concise definition of the purpose of firing a rocket. Unfortunately the term has become corrupted by people who have no knowledge of its provenance and, like so many good ideas branded with a ridiculous title, it has developed into a fatuous, misunderstood exercise that is now seen as a method of extolling things that slick managers would like others to believe about them and their companies.

Don't fall into that trap. Use the exercise to establish what it is that your business does in simple terms without flowery or pompous consultant-speak. What you are trying to do is define what your business should do and how it should do it – nothing more. And make the language as brutal as you like. The purpose of any commercial business can be reduced to one thing ultimately – the making of profits. Corporate psycho-babble about acting morally, nurturing employees and behaving properly towards the community used to disguise true intentions of grinding competitors into the ground, can be indulged in if you really want to when you are flying straight and level, on course and near to being home. At the moment your job is to plan a course for survival.

Assemble the information about the wider market; look at what your competitors are doing right and learn from them; analyse what your customers want from you. Now set about putting the essence of what you have learned into practice by writing down a very simple set of targets for each part of the business – profit centre or cost centre. This target structure can usually be divided into three parts: first, holding existing customers; second, expanding the volume of sales to existing customers; and third, finding new customers.

This classification has a direct link to the expansion of turnover since there are usually three ways of developing turnover profitably:

the first is to sell more of what you are already selling to your existing customers;

the second is to sell something different to your existing customer base;

the third is to sell what you already sell to a different customer.

Of these tacks the first is very much to be preferred since it can be applied more quickly and more easily and involves fewer introductory costs than the other two options. If you are going to construct a plan that shows real increases in unit turnover as being your salvation then you should probably use the first option as being the one most likely to succeed.

Establish, in consultation with your senior managers, what these simple targets should be, then get them to write their own plans for how they intend to achieve these targets. The miniplans should be written on the basis of two assumptions: first, what they would need to accomplish the targets with no unreasonable restriction of resources (and how long it would take them to achieve the targets); and second, how they would go about achieving their targets with the resources they currently have in hand, again giving an indication of the time involved. The restricted resources version of the plan is the one that you are going to use but the reason for doing both is that it is very much easier to think how you might ideally go about doing something and then work your way back rather than to do it the other way round.

This approach can and should be applied steadily to all the areas of the business – even cost centres can actively contribute to this list if the right perception of the business is developed. For instance, accounts sections can help consolidate existing customers by ensuring accounts are accurately and consistently dealt with; they can assist in expanding sales to existing customers by providing the sales department with accurate information about costing, margins and discounts for size; and they can help develop new markets by providing special help in the costing and development of prototypes and innovative financing structures.

By doing these three things – analysing the main market that you serve, looking at your competitors, and then thinking of your own business's goals – you may well discover areas of the market-place that you had not entered before: customers you have not served; products you have not previously thought of selling; types of sale that you have not undertaken. You may also begin to look at your business in a new way so that the route for recovery is seen more clearly.

This process can appear daunting. It is often very time-consuming and if it is to be successful it requires that effort be devoted to planning a path forward for the next few months just at a time when the way that the next day is going to pan out is very unclear. However, it is one of the few areas where paid help can be obtained reasonably cheaply by enlisting the help of the local Business Link. These bodies have funds for helping companies to employ consultants who can assist in working out new marketing plans or determining which new skills may be required if a change in the direction of the business is undertaken. While this help usually requires some form of matching funding from the company, it may be an option that should be explored as a method of implementing change rapidly in an area where few small company management teams are well equipped.

The same principles apply to employing professional help in this field as in any other (see Chapter 13 on accountants' investigations). You will get more out of the exercise at both lower cost and less disruption if you understand very clearly what you want from the professionals involved and if they understand what you want from them. Have a very clear understanding of what it is that you are looking for professional help to contribute before you start paying for that help to come in to advise you. There is an old adage that consultants are very good at taking your watch and telling you the time and charging you a lot for the privilege. That is certainly true of consultants badly instructed and badly handled by their commissioning clients. Good consultants, properly instructed, will know that your aim is to be able to tell the time: they will find you a good watch, show you how it works and *then* charge you a lot for doing it. But the difference is that you will have something worthwhile to use in your business once they have left.

Key points

1. The proper appreciation of the market that you want to exploit is the key to sustained future growth.

2. This is probably the origin of the mistakes of the past that contributed to bringing the business down.

3. Rebuild your market appreciation by tapping as many sources of information as you can and using your own internally generated information as probably the most reliable source – for all its shortcomings. Do not neglect to use informal sources like sales staff opinions.

4. Shut down, strip out or otherwise eliminate all marketing and production activities that do not contribute directly to the exploitation of the market you have aimed your business at.

5. Focus your business very strictly on what it is that it should be doing but avoid over-intellectualising the purpose or up-ending the correct priorities through flabby management-textbook-style thinking. The purpose is to make money; everything else is a secondary consideration, given the situation in which you find yourself.

6. Seek help if you feel that the capabilities of the management team are not up to a detailed revamping of the marketing plan; while it may not be possible for you to employ expensive consultants, Business Links may have (limited) funds to help kick-start the process.

Chapter 7

The plan for recovery

You now have a mass of information, opinions and suggestions about the business that you are trying to recover, derived from the analyses and consultation exercises you have done. Certain actions may already have been taken because they could not wait for the results of a longer review. You may have disposed of bits of the business, sold some or all of the company car fleet; got rid of some of the staff who were obviously not going to be able to participate effectively in recovering the business.

You have generated sufficient cash to keep your company going while you came to this point or found sufficient temporary resources left in the creditors/debtors and bank account to stretch you this far. You may have done nothing (unlikely!), trusting that the situation was not so bad that you could not afford to wait until the information you needed was available.

Now is the time to organise that information into a coherent plan that you will use to navigate your way out of the problems that the business faces. This plan will be both for internal consumption and action and also the commercial equivalent of your 'flight plan'. You are going to use it to tell the bankers and accountants (and possibly even suppliers) whose help you are going to need where you want to go, how you expect to get there and whereabouts you expect to be at any given time. You are going to aviate, navigate and communicate with this plan.

Whichever of these actions you have taken or not taken, you are still aviating. So at this point you should make a final decision about whether or not you can realistically start to navigate and communicate – in other words, whether you think that you have a chance of being able to recover the business. If you can legitimately decide that you can drag the business back from the brink and generate real value in the business by growing it thereafter – even if only with the help of further financing from the bank or shareholders or from forbearing suppliers (on the basis of a persuasive case) – then you should go ahead and develop the plan further in the expectation that you can persuade the necessary resources out of those involved.

If you can only see your way to recovery by experiencing a massive increase in sales from an unidentifiable source or by employing a further increase in debt with no evidence of any collateral (real assets brought in from some source currently available) to support it – then you should not waste your time further. What you have decided is that finding your way home and a possible mid-air refuelling is not enough; you have really concluded that you want to change planes and change routes.

So, if you decide that you can continue, you are now about to begin aviating *and* navigating in seriousness. The additional work involved in aviating and navigating is substantial and the incremental load in aviating, navigating and communicating is even heavier – so at this point you will have to begin adopting a number of roles and also to begin to delegate extensively.

Since it is crucially important for you now to *control* the recovery you cannot avoid passing most of the responsibility for *getting things done* to the rest of the management team. The plan should be yours – compiled with the compete participation of the management team; the execution of it will be theirs – under your direction.

But we are getting slightly ahead of ourselves and into the province of the next chapter. What you must now do with this collection of information you have derived from the work you have done so far is to organise it into a plan – a route out of the unknown and back into flyable conditions – that you can use to persuade others to offer you further resources, as well as for your own navigation. This plan is going to be completely unique to your business, so trying to indicate the contents in detail is an impossibility. But we can indicate the content in broad terms.

The first thing to say about the plan is that it should have an objective that can be framed in very simple language. It should say something like 'The objective for XYZ Co. is to produce widgets of the highest quality at the lowest possible cost within a period of — months.' This lets everyone, inside the business and outside, know where you are going and gives a rationale for all the future actions that you take. Measure all your future actions against this statement – if the proposed action does not fit this objective then do not do it. But beware of the bland stupidities of the portmanteau 'mission statement'.

The second thing to say is that the plan should be short. It should probably extend to no more than five or six pages of text at the maximum. The best way to order the text is to use as much as possible of the information that you have derived in its original form. That which you wish to use in support of your argument should be put into appendices – not included as clutter in the body of the plan. Remember, your plan will be judged as a route for getting you from where you are (unsafe) to where you want to be (safe). It does not have to be either voluminous or of prize-winning literary quality but it does have to be accurate, concise and complete. If you are boarding a flight at an airport you expect to know the destination, at what time the flight will leave, when it will arrive, what other airports it might call at and how much it will cost. If you were controlling the flight from the ground you would also want to know where the flight might be at any given time so that you could track it accurately. Your company flight plan should contain all these things too if it is to be of any real use to you and to others.

The last chapter suggested that at some late point in the market evaluation you should prepare, in combination with your senior managers, a series of targeted miniplans for the individual component departments that make up your business. These miniplans, once agreed and fully documented, should form the basis of the overall plan that you run the business by and the document that you give to bankers or shareholders to elicit their support. Embroider it as little as possible when presenting it to others; the simpler the better as far as setting realistic targets is concerned.

Successful navigation is about the accurate tracking of time and heading. Using these two components you can work out where you are if you know your starting point. Your starting point is fixed – it is the one fixed point that you are sure of! – so the plan establishes the heading; it gives you the direction in which you wish to go. If you add to the heading a number of waypoints by which you can evaluate how well you are doing, and which if implemented will bring about a restoration of fortunes, you will have established the basics of the navigational plan for recovering the company.

The most important part of the plan for recovery is that it should contain indications of *when* things are going to happen and *when* results will show – these are the points that you need to know so that you can monitor the time component of your plan to give you an indication of where you should be along your recovery route. The importance of this is that it provides three things: first, a ready measure for evaluation of the success or failure of what you are trying to do; second, a series of prompts for initiating actions and following them up; and third, it gives the managers involved a complete programme of what is expected of them and when. Since they were also active participants in the compilation of the plan it also gives them nowhere to hide from their responsibilities!

An example might help to illustrate these points. For instance, the miniplan for the manufacturing section of a small company might include the following among the waypoints it established:

XYZ Products Co., manufacturing section miniplan

TARGET
Increase the usable output of the department by 5 per cent within two months.

EFFECT
Improvement in margin of c.£12,000 annually; c.£1,000 per month.

METHOD
1. Improvement in working drawings.
   Date of implementation: by 31 October.
   Responsible: Operations director.
2. Increased supervisory attention.
   Date of implementation: immediate.
   Responsible: Foreman.
3. Better training of staff.
   Date of Implementation: on identification of particular individual training needs or by 31 October.
   Responsible: Personnel manager.
4. Introduction of bonus scheme (to be self-financing) based on reduction in wastage costs over month.
   Date of implementation: by 1 September.
   Responsible: Finance director.

This type of format indicates what you want to do; when you expect to have it implemented and what the expected results are. By building up such miniplans for the company as a whole, the planning process is achieved in easily manageable lumps – falling into our basic approach towards all big problems of reducing them to a size where they can be coped with.

There is no point in tweaking a good and realistic plan to try to make the results come through faster. Unrealistic planning will only produce grief later as the results apparently come through slowly (in reality at the pace which should have been included in the plan) and the scheduling goes awry as sequencing and control become more and more difficult to track. A solid plan, realistically constructed, that can be kept to, will be far better received as a proposal by a banker than a spectacular recovery plan that is missed.

What you do have to be prepared for – and so must the people to whom you are presenting the plan – is that the impact of the changes that you are going to make will begin to diminish in volume as time goes by. You can make bigger impacts initially because you are taking big crude actions to make large changes; as the weeks go on, the effects get smaller simply because you have probably tackled the easy, biggest problems first.

You must not allow yourself or your management team to get discouraged by this. The fact that the actions you are taking are getting finer and finer and that their effect is less and less marked is a sign that things are getting better. Think of it in aviating terms: the control inputs needed to make the plane fly straight and level are much less than those needed to pull it out of a violent manoeuvre.

This will have to be borne in mind when you prepare your recovery plan for presentation to the bank. Bankers see lots of recovery plans and being sceptical is the easy option for them. You will have to show that your recovery plan is solidly founded and properly constructed. Furthermore, unless you have had a wholesale clearance of the management team, you will be asking the banker to back a group of managers that has already failed to perform competently (in the bank's eyes) and yet which, with an unrealistic plan, you will be indicating can perform miracles of production, marketing and administration of the sort they have never been capable of before. Not very convincing.

Dressing the plan up is a completely different thing, of course, from making sure that there is no excess fat in the estimates given of when things can be done and when results can be expected. Watch out that individuals responsible for implementation of the plans do not give themselves unreasonable latitude; your own investigations should have enabled you to detect padding or those who are likely to indulge in padding.

You should satisfy yourself that the plans submitted to you are realistic when they come from the individual authors – the directors and other members of the management team responsible for the individual departmental plans – since you will be placing your reputation on the block when you take the plan to the bank. That means that you should be as sure that there is no overenthusiasm or overeagerness about reporting the likely impact of results as you are about not understating their effect: each is going to be bad for your case in the long run (although in different ways – you could find that you have raised too much money, thereby paying too much in interest charges or releasing too much equity) if the results of your plan turn out differently from what you have publicised.

The intricacies of dealing with bankers are dealt with in a later chapter; it is enough to say at this point that a judicial openness is the best policy. The same does not *necessarily* always go for your own dealings with the management team. While the majority of decisions must be taken in a spirit of complete openness and truthfulness if there is going to be any hope of the recovery succeeding, there will be certain matters which must be left to you alone. The effects of unforeseen events in the recovery may force you to cut the jobs of senior managers in order to save costs and it is a pointless exercise to have these publicised in specific detail in advance. You cannot sensibly discuss the theoretical detail of an event that may cost an employee their job prior to the event happening. It will merely adversely affect their ability to do their job. And in the situation, which you face together, everyone will already be aware that continued failure to perform of the business as a whole will result in job losses.

In order to prepare for these eventualities, you should have a subordinate plan available for your own purposes which will give you the choice of a number of options in the event that things do not turn out the way that the plan suggests. This plan should be a sketch map, not a detailed route map, for your own purposes, indicating what things could be done at any given point, in terms of costed actions to be taken to try to salvage the situation.

For instance, should you fail to win a large order crucial to the cash-flow you have predicted, you should have in mind what actions this ought to prompt. The loss of an order worth £200,000 which should have been won at 40 per cent gross margin might mean that you have to lose two shop-floor workers or one salesperson, for example. The alternative might be, say, that you have to defer the introduction of some new computer design equipment, jeopardising securing another contract, resulting in even more job losses in the long run.

You will have to know what these alternatives are so that you can give a lead in the discussions that will follow a setback and so that the whole of your plan is not thrown into turmoil by one gear not clicking into position at the expected time. It will also provide a good example to your colleagues and enhance the likelihood of you getting your own way in arguments about the right course to follow (reducing the time spent in needlessly studying the subject from every angle) if you have a good alter-native route mapped out for as many eventualities as you can foresee.

The preparation for this work should be done while the initial cash-flows are being prepared. Questions about the effect of a £30,000, £40,000 or £100,000 shortfall in revenue on the viability of staffing levels, or even the business itself, are easily disguised at that moment whereas they can excite rumour later at a time when rumours are deeply damaging and – of course – distressing to those who might be affected by them. (The effect of good morale in the recovery of a business should not be neglected and is a subject to which we shall return in Chapter 14.)

This additional plan should concentrate on personnel matters against a financial background. (You might also consider the possibility and timing of a crash landing, see Chapter 12.) It should help you to decide who goes and who stays when you have to play the Balloon Game and toss people out. It should also remind you of what additional resources you might need as you go along.

In particular you should be prepared to change your mind about an individual's worth to the business in the light of changing evidence about their performance. Initial prejudices, positive or negative, can be costly if they are not occasionally reviewed in the light of circumstances.

This obviously leads on to the next admonition: you are now in control of the recovery so you have to control the implementation of the plan. The actual doing of the actions that you have determined is up to your management team. That is the subject of the next chapter.

Key points

1. Draw the information that you have gathered together into a brief plan, your 'flight plan' for recovery telling all who need to know where you are going; how you are going to get there; and at what time you expect to arrive.

2. The plan should be based on your individual departmental miniplans.

3. It should be kept as brief and factual as possible.

4. It should contain details of the timing of events, actions and results so that you can keep track of where you are going.

5. You should be the controller of the plan from here on in since that is the best way of occupying your time. From now on, delegate action to others.

Chapter 8

Delegating the flying

In getting this far, you have kept the business going by doing two things: first, establishing the immediate top priority requirements of continuing to trade (and implementing what needs to be done immediately); and second, working down to the operational level by sorting out miniplans for individual sections of the business. Using our flying analogy, you have continued to aviate; by putting the plans in place you have begun to navigate, and now you must continue that process and start to communicate as well.

The overall requirements of the business have been relatively easy to ascertain – the principal problem will have been the generation of cash. If you have got this far then you have probably got at least some of the way to sorting that out, even if you have not solved it.

The miniplans that you have already constructed will give a good basis for developing the recovery of the business. They are robust at the operational level, since they assign targets to identifiable parts of the business and then allocate responsibilities to specific individuals for getting those things done. They are designed to improve their performance and so win custom, increase revenue and improve profitability – thereby all contributing to the correction of the first, and overriding, problem of cash availability. The top of the problem and the bottom of the problem have therefore been dealt with and the chosen solutions will reinforce each other. What remains to be tackled is the middle section of the problem, the managerial problem.

We have already noted that one of the features of a business that is experiencing difficulties is that some jobs get left undone while others are 'overdone' as everyone tries to pitch in. This confusing tendency, with everyone their own managing director/sales director/finance director, is one of the contributing factors to the incipient further decline of the business. It can be more or less halted in its tracks by an application of common sense – even though unravelling the effects of it may take a little longer.

That application of common sense has to come from you. It does not involve anything particularly hard to understand, any advanced management theory or any special training. It does involve you reviewing the organization chart of the business to make sure that it makes sense. Once you have done this you go on to deciding who is to do what by allocating specific responsibilities for specific tasks within a specific period of time and then ensuring that they are carried out.

In short, it requires someone to take a lead in sorting out the confusion that is generated by the uncertainty prevalent in a business that is temporarily out of control. That lead has to come from you. It is now the *only* thing that you can sensibly do since there will not be enough hours in the day to sort out by yourself the application of the plans that you have decided on as a management team. There is absolutely no sense in deciding on a plan as a *group* of managers, which presupposes that a *group* of managers will be available to execute it, and then to abandon that primary assumption by trying to do everything yourself. Delegation is the key to the next stage of the exercise. By harnessing the energies of individual managers in a directed way as a co-ordinated group, much more will be achieved than by rushing around being individual busy fools together. Remember, however, the first rule: there can only ever be one pilot-in-command.

Delegation means that you have to control the activities of the senior managers just as you expect them to control the activities of the mini-plans within their individual areas of responsibility. Remember that as far as you are concerned controlling does *not* mean undertaking – unless, of course, part of the specific remit that you give yourself is actually to execute some part of the activity that you have taken responsibility for.

Above all, you must avoid trying to do someone else's job once you have tasked them with it. If you do interfere you will be compounding the problem that contributed to bringing the business down, one that, if left unchecked, will also bring you down: that is the problem of interference in areas of specialist responsibility that unqualified or untasked individuals should be steering clear of. You will also be wasting your most precious resource – time – and either frustrating a perfectly competent operator or damaging the confidence of someone who might become a perfectly competent operator.

You must bear in mind the damage that you will do to the morale of the whole organisation by developing a reputation as an interferer, even though the temptation to 'help out' may be very strong. Leave to those whom you have allocated tasks the carrying out of those tasks.

If you are uncertain about the abilities of someone to do the job which they are supposed to be doing then you should either give the job to someone else to do (still denying yourself the latitude for interference) and retask the individual about whom you have doubts, or remove the weak link from the chain entirely. You cannot afford, given what is at stake, to rely on someone whose performance may be substandard, provided always that you have the ability to reorganise your resources in such a way that the genesis of a further problem will be avoided. You are in the business of reducing problems for yourself, not creating more. Decisive action now concerning the suitability of someone to do the tasks required will save you much heartache later, even though it may be a difficult decision to execute at the time. It will also be kinder to the individual involved and to the remaining members of the team whose future fortunes depend upon the quality of the decisions that you make now.

Unfortunately, in making this decision your options are going to be limited since, by definition, you do not have endless resources of cash, time or personnel to use in differing combinations to apply to all the tasks that need to be done. One of the biggest problems facing any small to medium-size business is the lack of resources at middle management level. Too often, people who should be directing the business are forced to act the role of middle managers. Occasionally the reverse happens and someone is promoted beyond their ability so that they become poor directors when really they would make excellent middle managers.

When serious commercial and financial problems arise of the sort that you are facing, this situation gets thrown into sharp relief. Those directors without competent or sufficient middle managers to support them get sucked into doing rather than directing. The poor quality directors – those who should really be managers – act as a drag on the speed of response of the rest of the directors because they have to be consulted, persuaded or cajoled to do things that the others can more quickly see the benefit of doing, or because they do not actually do the jobs that their positions nominally qualify them for, leaving pieces of the operation undone for others to pick up. They may even try to alter the route adopted by the business by retracing decisions that have been taken collectively and taking further unauthorised decisions that do not accord with the policy that has been agreed upon.

In this situation, where there are not enough competent directors to run all the roles required, you have three options, none of which is perfect.

Option one is to get rid of the director – which may be very difficult because of the legal and financial impact of so doing – and promote someone competent to fill their place.

Option two is to work round the problem by effectively freezing the individual out of crucial matters of policy implementation (while still keeping them informed of what is going on) and relegating them to the implementation of less crucial subordinate tasks while other staff are used to effect policy decisions or the work is shared out among the remaining directors. This choice is usually only acceptable where there is someone you cannot get rid of for institutional reasons – a director with a major shareholding, say, or the proprietor's son, for instance.

Option three breaks the rule about interference by working with the individual involved so that you oversee their activities very closely. If you do this, you may choose to increase the frequency of reporting on the implementation of tasks to a level much above what you accept from other competent directors, for instance. Either the director or manager subjected to this option will find the situation intolerable and leave, or the close attention that you pay to the problem will result in success.

It should be clear that the option chosen to deal with the problem will have to depend upon the specifics of the situation and the characteristics of the individual involved. None of the options will be ideal and all will involve costs in terms of time and duplication of effort – some might even involve actual cash costs.

The situation is complicated further because there is an unfortunate inherent confusion of roles in the title 'director' as a result of the differing legal, commercial and even sociological connotations that the word has. Striking the correct balance between doing and directing is a very difficult task in an environment where the continuing existence of a business is precariously balanced, even for a good director who knows what should be done and is equipped to do the job intellectually and by experience. For an individual who has achieved the 'status' of a director it can only be seen as a retrograde step to lose that title – a view reinforced by the implicit view that the law takes, that directors are automatically competent – even if the amount of actual help that such a removal would give to the business might well secure the continued employment of that director in the longer run.

Here the aviating allusion may be of help again. Everyone on board an aircraft in an operating capacity is 'aircrew'; but they are not all 'pilots'. One member of the crew takes responsibility for piloting the plane; another takes responsibility for looking after the engines; a third takes responsibility for navigation; yet another looks after the passengers. In a crisis, the engineer does not swap roles with the pilot or try to tell the pilot which way to steer. Nor is the crew member who looks after passengers suddenly asked to take over the piloting of the plane. The safe operation of the aircraft flying to its destination is based on the delegation of aeronautical activities under the control of the pilot, *with all the members of the crew doing their allocated tasks to the best of their ability*. The allusion can be transferred to the situation of a business without too much effort but its effective implementation is not quite so easy, since the aeronautical tradition of semi-automatic deference to the pilot is not accorded to the managing director in quite the same measure.

The most effective way of deciding who shall do what is to sort out priorities in discussion with the directors and senior managers involved – and this can be achieved by forming small teams to decide on major priorities and then increasing the range, the scope and the depth of those priorities amongst other members of the business's staff in a sort of cascade of increasing activity. In other words, the same principle as was adopted in preparing and implementing the departmental miniplans will work for allocating tasks and responsibilities among the directors.

Finding the time to do this sorting out is a major problem for many businesses in trouble. How is it possible to find time in a day already over-packed with pressing priorities to sort out responsibilities and allocate tasks? The answer is that time for this activity has to be made available if the problem is to be overcome. Organise a working lunch; hold a regular morning meeting before the business of the day starts; have an hour set aside at the end of the day when the staff have gone home. The instilling of the discipline required to make even one day fit what you want to do with it will be part of the solution to the problems that beset the business.

There is a siren call in this process that says that the best way to make more time available is to throw more bodies at the problem: recruit more people to do the jobs that need to be done; put in more hours to complete the tasks. Apart from the fact that these approaches all take cash to implement – one of the resources that is in short supply in your situation – there is no purpose in compounding the problem by adding to the confusion over who does what, how and by when, because you have not thought out what you should be doing.

To bring about the necessary changes, it is necessary artificially to create a temporary vacuum in the business, a gap between managing and directing – but definitely not between *managers* and *directors* – so that the correct solution comes in to fill that vacuum. That will mean that the directors will have to take an objective look at the way they perform their own roles and think very carefully about what the business truly needs from them and from the resources which it currently deploys.

The key to doing this is metaphorically to rebuild the business on a blank sheet of paper, using only the people resources currently available to it and redeploying individuals among the various tasks required for the business to perform effectively, if their abilities allow it. In fact, this could be the best use of a blank piece of paper that you ever undertake. Find a large blank sheet of paper and set down an organisation chart with names and responsibilities attached. Crucial gaps will almost certainly be revealed, as will overcapacity – if it exists – in certain areas.

This need not be a long exercise, or one which involves prolonged analysis: in a relatively small and uncomplicated business, a morning could well see the exercise completed. But it does require a willingness to jettison preconceptions about the business and to think about it in a fresh way without the accumulated encrustation of experience – although that having been said, a leavening of experience can help avoid the traps that a flat, theoretical approach would lay for the innocent.

This process should lead to the scrapping of any unnecessary activity in the business, paving the way for a cleaner organisation chart and simplified structure which might make better use of skills and abilities embedded in the business. The process will then reveal two further things: the skills and resources that are absent from the business at the moment and, with a bit of further thinking, the resources and skills that are required of existing employees and directors as the business expands. This will then allow evaluations to be made of the suitability of individuals – senior managers *and* directors – for coping with the anticipated growth.

You may well find once you have done this that you want to initiate training plans for some of your key members of staff so that they can cope better with the requirements of their jobs, as newly defined. This will require money to do effectively but it is the one thing that you should think about squeezing into your survival budget if you can, since it is effectively protecting the likelihood of future growth. There is also the possibility that you can attract some funding from the local government-sponsored agency to help you with certain types of training.

Once you have completed an assessment of skill levels, performance targets and training requirements you should accompany this with a written job description (see also Chapter 5).

Undertaking a skills and competence audit – which is effectively what you will have analysed once you have finished the exercise – will help you to conduct the reviews of staff performance effectively when you get around to doing that in the next three months or so after the business has been stabilised. You will have generated a platform, in discussion with the individuals involved, that will enable you to assess and evaluate subsequent performance over the appropriate period.

Once you have established the new structure of management – which may or may not be different from what existed in the past – you must follow it up by regular formal reviews that consider what has been done from meeting to meeting and evaluate progress towards the overall targets that you have jointly established. But do not be frightened of holding irregular and informal reviews of progress if this seems to be appropriate. You must avoid the temptation of interference if your overall strategy is going to come good, but that does not mean that once the strategy has been established you should hide behind the walls of your plan to the detriment of day-to-day consideration of changes in the business environment. You are not in a position to do the day-to-day management of the business operation once the plans have been set but you are supposed to be making sure that minor changes to the plans are being accommodated as the situation requires. To go back to the aviation analogy, once the plane is flying along a more or less steady course, the pilot turns attention to checking that waypoints along the route are being passed at the appropriate times and that the predicted height and speed are being maintained; adjustments to the controls are now confined to those minor inputs required to maintain the flight plan.

So you should now adopt the strategy of the cinematic airline pilots: every so often you should stretch your legs by going for a walk around, nodding to the passengers, checking that the cabin crew are doing their job properly – and making sure that the wings and tail are still in place.

Management by walking about is something of an out-of-fashion management concept but not all the best practice needs to be validated by the dictates of fashion. There is a lot to be said for seeing and being seen inside a business and you should make sure that you do not wall yourself up in an ivory tower while you formulate and execute your plans. By isolating yourself from the day-to-day dynamics of the business you risk losing the 'feel' of it and you will get a much better idea of the way that the business is running and whether the plans which you are considering are workable if you keep in touch with the mood on the shop-floor or in the accounts office or among the field sales force.

Key points

1. Now that you have got this far you must turn your attention to the management of the business rather than the management of the cashflow.

2. Review your organisation chart thoroughly and delegate tasks, duties and functions to individuals cleanly, matching their competences against the needs of the business.

3. Eliminate weak links in the management chain now. A modest application of ruthlessness as to the abilities of individuals at this point will save much grief later.

4. Resist at all costs the temptation to interfere with the execution of tasks by those to whom you have delegated them. Cut individuals out of the decision-making or executive processes if they cannot be removed from the structure for some reason; supervise them more closely or put them to different tasks. But do not waste time and effort and reduce morale by meddling, manipulating or interfering.

5. Keep in touch with what is going on outside the immediate confines of the management team.

Chapter 9

Managerial information, the crucial input

Believe your eyes and what the instruments tell you.
CAPTAIN TREVOR THOM, *THE AIR PILOT'S MANUAL*

You will have concluded long before now that accurate, timely and relevant information about how your business is doing is vital to your ability to control the course of the business and its recovery. When you step back from actually doing things yourself to a role where you supervise others – as you must at some point if the recovery is going to succeed – it becomes even more important that you have good information with which to monitor the progress of the recovery. (For most of this chapter we shall be considering only the financial aspect of management information. The business, whether stable or recovering, can be steered by reference to this alone for a brief while. But it should not be forgotten that a complete management information system will take into account other developments in the environment in which the business operates – and needs to do so if it is to continue to prosper. The financial aspect is only one facet of a complete system. Other elements will be treated separately in other chapters.)

There are three qualifying adjectives used above in connection with financial management information about a business: accurate; timely; relevant. We shall return to expand on the importance of these characteristics later when we consider some of the desirable features that might be included in a new management information system, but their significance should be borne in mind at all times in considering the value of information.

Without proper (that is, accurate, timely and relevant) information you will be completely unable to determine whether the actions you have taken are having the effects that you anticipated or whether new influences on your company's activities have to be accommodated in your plans. Not least, without proper reporting of information, some of the 'feel' of events that can help a manager to anticipate changes and responses necessary to control activity is lost when responsibility for implementation passes to others. Just as a pilot will want to feel the immediate responses of the aircraft to the way the stick and rudder are moved, so you need to know as quickly as possible what changes are happening in the business by way of reaction to the things that you have put in train.

So it is of absolute importance to the continuation of the recovery that you make sure that the information you receive from your managerial systems is as good (accurate and relevant) as it possibly can be – and, just as important, that it is as timely as you need it. You will have appreciated from the initial work you have done in bringing the business to this point, that stale information is no good to anyone. In fact it is positively dangerous – the time spent in collecting it means that effort has been wasted which could have been put to better purpose. It is better not to try to produce information that is going to be of no use in controlling a business than to waste time and effort in doing so. (And as we shall see below, one of the actions in designing a new management information system is to weed out what you do not want.)

The only thing that is worse than late information is information which is wrong – and when information gets stale it becomes wrong by definition (for the purposes of current decision-making at least) since events will have passed it by. In fact, overextended timing for the collection and analysis of data is perhaps another one of the symptoms that could be suggested as being indicators of a company in trouble.

You will be able to bring about recovery only if you have the information systems that enable you to chart your progress and make necessary and inevitable alterations to your business plan and the way that the business is run. But in the situation in which you find yourself, building the systems will be one of your primary tasks since, as we have already suggested, it is more than likely that a failure of information systems contributed to the wider problems of the business in the first place. You are placed in the paradox that you need time to build the system to help the business recover but having the system there already *is* one of the best ways of buying yourself some time to help the business recover (since you will be making good decisions based on proper information and not bad ones based on poor information). So you go round in circles.

And the circle may be made tighter by the fact that the people you are now working with may be the operators of the poor systems and so are perhaps tainted with the failings of the past.

The only course of action in such circumstances is to make a start somewhere in order to break out of the problem. It is, anyway, unrealistic to expect that a new information system can be born overnight and equally impractical to anticipate that there is nothing in the existing system which is worth keeping. A piecemeal approach to change, tempered by a widespread understanding throughout the organisation that changes are necessary to ensure the salvation of the business, is likely to be the most profitable path to follow. This should bring about a critical review of the existing system and its failings by the management and help speed the progress in making changes; in addition, if the managers involved are worth keeping, their energies will be harnessed to the process of change.

Whether or not the business is ready for you to back away from doing things yourself and pass tasks over to your colleagues is a question that can only be decided by the application of your judgement rather than any objective appraisal. As a practical problem it inevitably involves some contamination by the chicken and egg dilemma. (It also involves considerations of management morale.) What is certain is that you will see the recovery you have nurtured falter if the information system that you are going to use to steer the business forward is not up to the task.

If the managers of a failing company do not appreciate the importance of data being converted into information in a swift way then they are unlikely to appreciate the rapidity with which the tide of events can swing against them. And if after realising that they have fallen into a trough of decline they are unable to see the need for improving the speed at which they collect information about their business and its markets, then they will probably have to be jettisoned from the business to make way for others who can appreciate the requirement.

In short, making a good information system your primary priority after you have stabilised the business will help you to solve a number of problems, not simply those of information management. It will also give you some rapid assessments of the calibre of the people that you are working with.

In order to set the structure for this, let us go back to the aviation analogy. Think what a pilot would do after pulling an aeroplane out of a steep dive: start by checking all the instruments to make sure that they were registering properly and that the initial, intuitive appreciation of airspeed, attitude, height, heading and fuel remaining were all correct in comparison with what the instruments were showing. The pilot would then keep on checking the instruments to make sure that they had not been affected by the violence of the manoeuvres just gone through.

And once the dynamics of the situation were clear, those five basic instruments – airspeed indicator, artificial horizon, altimeter, compass and fuel gauge – would help pilot the plane safely to its destination.

You have been through the commercial equivalent of the aeroplane's steep dive. You have just pulled out and now you are going to have to make sure that your instruments give you sensible readings so that you keep flying straight and level along the track that you have plotted. However, unlike the pilot's five basic instruments, you have only three basic ones that you must watch: profit and loss, balance sheet and cashflow.

But the task is not so simple as merely keeping an eye on the instruments. There are a number of ways to measure profit that are equally valid; pinning down margins can require very complex measurement, and cashflows can be shown in many formats. So you have the added complication that there are very different ways for different businesses to collect information on the same quantity – the pilot has only the resulting measurements that the instruments show to be concerned with and does not have to try to work out the best way to collect the information while flying, as you will probably have to do.

In addition to trying to determine which is the best way to collect the information that you need, you will also have to decide what unnecessary information to filter out. A large part of your job in determining the shape and structure of your new management information system will be to reduce the amount of information coming to you to a sensible level so that you avoid the situation where you are overloaded with information and paralysed by analysis. The old system that you have inherited is probably either too sparse to provide the basics for sensible management decisions or is clogged up because too much of the wrong sort of information was collected.

However, the three basic groups of information – profit and loss, cashflow and balance sheet – *if checked against each other*, will provide you with the indicators you need for steering yourself to safety. But you must check them against each other and not become fixated with one or the other.

The pilot is taught to depend upon the instruments, no matter what they show, for taken together they will always tell the truth, so long as they are all scanned frequently. Flying blind in bad weather or at night, if something seems wrong then the instruments must be believed and adjustments made accordingly. But the pilot has to take the complete picture that the instruments show and not rely on just one in isolation.

Very much the same is true in a businessman. If something *seems* intuitively wrong when taken in comparison with other measures, then the chances are better than evens that it *is* wrong – even if the isolated measure of activity shows a reasonable reading. If the profit and loss account looks good but does not tie up with cashflow as it should, then *something is wrong*. If the balance sheet looks increasingly unhealthy and does not show the changes that you would expect from cashflow results that have been recorded, then *something is wrong*. If you have been making good profits but the business is eating cash, then *something is wrong*. And you must do something about it.

The quickest way to do this is to improve the quality, and perhaps the quantity, of management information coming to you. So you are going to have to rebuild your management information system.

Building a new information system

Any system of financial information for a business, no matter how complicated or how simple, has to be designed as a triangle. It has to have three basic points that allow accurate cross-checking. If we go back again to our basic analogy of piloting a plane, accurate navigation can only be done if you have three points of reference:

- you must know where you started from;
- you must know where you are (which may be the same point as where you started from, of course);
- and you must know where you want to be.

In fact, more generally, you can accurately determine your point in any plane (the geometric type) only if you can triangulate your position by using three points of cross-reference. Plotting the course for a business also involves a sort of financial triangulation if an accurate result is to be achieved. As we have already seen, the triangulation points in company financial information are the profit and loss account, the cashflow and the balance sheet.

You need not confine yourself to these three pieces of information, of course. They are to be regarded as a minimum requirement and the principal concern – aside from the overriding considerations of accuracy, relevance and timeliness – must always be to select measures and gather information that are helpful to the needs of the business.

However, it is unlikely that unelaborated P&L accounts, balance sheet and cashflow would be enough to control the business precisely. Except for the simplest of businesses, some further form of analysis is almost certain to be desirable. A gross turnover figure at the top of the P&L account is unlikely to be a satisfactory indication of the way that sales are moving unless it is broken down further in some form of subsidiary analysis; an undifferentiated analysis of cost of sales that does not distinguish between raw materials costs and labour costs will probably not be adequate for steering the recovery course. For a multiproduct business, gross margin is best split between product lines rather than lumped together where it can hide problems in one product area. And so on.

When you begin to think of the detail of what you want of a financial information system, it is important to think simply. Think of the information that you *need* to control the business rather than of elaborate measures that might come in useful simply to show how deeply you can

mine information. As your first pass at the problem, think of the recovery
business plan that you have developed and try to match the financial
information system to the monitoring requirements of that *for an outsider*.
Remember that *information* starts its life as data and only becomes usable
after sensible analysis. If you overload the analytical circuitry you get back
to data again.

This does not mean that you should artificially limit your requirements to the basics. But consider what the old information system
usefully produced, plunder the best and the workable from that and fill in
any remaining gaps with your own requirements.

There is a second good reason for not overturning the existing
management information system entirely, and that is to do with staff
morale. Rubbishing the old system will inevitably lead to a decline in self-
esteem among those who were operating it (it is, after all, very unlikely
that *everything* was being done wrong) and will probably leave them
slightly adrift for some time while they get to grips with the new system.
Retaining elements of the old system and building on it with the new will
smooth the changeover. But be very careful that you weed out old practices in collecting information or processing it that needlessly complicate
the process of analysis or render it less robust.

You should demand what you want to receive from the system to suit
your own requirements in steering the business forward. Do not put up
with anything less than what you want, although you may have to accept
that you cannot have it all at once – changing systems costs time and
effort and you may be better off with a rough equivalence to what you
would like ideally, rather than have the accounts section tied up for days
in devising new, 'perfect', ways of recording information. If you cannot
get what you need without tearing the system apart and indulging in
some huge rebuilding – with consequently huge organisational costs –
look for 'proxies' in the information that you already collect.

For instance, it may be impractical to collect information on profitability in a certain period of time if the full range of information that is
required to give an accurate answer is too difficult to analyse or if the
accounting system is known to be deficient or corrupt in some particular
way as far as information collection is concerned. But cash generated or
consumed during the same period may be used as a rough proxy since
the combined effects of profit and working capital changes amount to
cashflow and if you can filter out working capital changes then the
resultant magnitude will give a rough indication of positive or negative
performance of profitability.

Often, simple information simply analysed gives a robust result that
will approximate to the more detailed and sophisticated analysis that
might take a lot longer to assemble and work through, especially if the
basic information collection system is unreliable or prone to distortion.

The flash result

It is worth remembering in the circumstances of the troubled company that speed of provision of information is vital, provided that the initial, provisional indication is going to be close to the final, more polished result. To this end you should develop a series of sturdy 'flash results' for your own purposes which give a simple and direct indication of how the business is performing. The minimum period of time to be spanned by these indicators is probably a week – although in the case of cash I suggest that you review the position daily so that you know what your likely overdraft position is at almost any given point.

These flash results will probably include the following:

- orders won during the week – but be careful to include only those accompanied by a purchase order and not those based on a salesperson's expectations;
- manufactured items completed during the week;
- cashflow in during the week – identified payments from customers;
- cashflow out during the week – identified payments to suppliers;
- resultant cash position at week end;
- debtors longer than 45 days at week end;
- anticipated production in week to come by volume and value;
- anticipated payments in;
- anticipated payments out;
- anticipated resultant cash position at week end.

It should come as no surprise that the list concentrates very heavily on cash as an indicator of the business's health. This is because cash is the most readily measurable financial item in a company – and the one that cannot lie. Profit is illusory; the balance sheet changes as soon as it is recorded. The cashflow tells the truth.

You may find that there is other information that you want to include; the list above is set out as a minimum requirement. For instance, you might want to have a weekly summary of turnover by category of sales, because you might know that unless your sales reach a certain level then you cannot make profits no matter what you do. You might want to know what new stock has been ordered and if the price has changed, so that you can judge the rate of likely materials consumption to give you an idea of manufacturing margin or to help predict likely pressure from creditors and cashflow in advance.

If you are trying to recover a business that is going through a very difficult cash time then you will certainly want to have a regular list of writs that are received by the business as creditors seek to recover their money. You will want to have a diary scheduling these and how they can be paid. Your short-term cashflow, which you will probably be revising every week, should certainly indicate these as a separate item.

What all this boils down to is that no set prescriptions can be offered: you will have to design your own system – your own instrument panel – to suit the requirements of your business. What you must remember in doing this, though, is that the information that you are seeking to develop must satisfy the three cardinal requirements that were listed at the start of this chapter – the information which you use for your decision making must be:

accurate;
relevant;
timely.

That means that the data from which it is derived must be:

readily available;
simple to collect;
not easily distorted by the process of analysis.

And whatever else you decide to analyse, you *must* have a good grip on cash since this is the company's single most precious resource next to time. Cash to a business is altitude indicator, fuel gauge, compass, attitude indicator and clock all rolled into one.

Three warnings need to be made here. First, in designing both your flash information system and your monthly accounts format, don't put up with information that is not suitable but has been squeezed to fit 'because we have always done it this way'. Information that has taken time to prepare but which you don't use or which is not suitable for your purpose has wasted cost, time and effort. You cannot afford to waste any of those.

Second, don't wait for information to confirm your intuition that you should have done something earlier. For instance, information about what materials were ordered a week ago may be accurate and reliable, but too late to be of any use in helping you to control cash consumption. You might be better off saying that there are discretionary limits to what can be ordered by subordinates without your written authority, so that you can control cash consumption at source – and, if necessary, cut off the tendency to over-order (and tie up cash in stocks of raw materials) at the root before it does any damage rather than after it is too late.

Third, make sure that you take note of what the information is telling you – promptly. As you will know from your initial investigations, one of the contributory factors to getting into difficulties in the first place was probably an absence of or disregard of critical information. Don't repeat the error, especially as getting this far has been so hard won. Making a

mistake is natural and forgivable; making the same mistake again is not
– it is simply careless.

Month-end analysis

As far as a more formal analysis is concerned, when designing a monthly
set of management information it is often very helpful to consider
employing the concept of the profit centre in working out how you want
to monitor progress. This loads all costs that can be attributed to
individual activities against their respective turnover. This can then be
used as a method of pushing responsibility for generating turnover
and controlling costs down the organisational tree to where it should
properly reside.

It has the advantage that eliminates places where managers can hide
behind the claim that a cost was someone else's responsibility and also
throws into relief the performance of good managers who can manage
their own areas of responsibility against the record of bad managers who
cannot. Far from being simply a crude tool with which to bludgeon
managers over the head, if used properly it can have the useful effect of
quickly indicating where cost and pricing problems lie in an organisation.

The following suggestions will give some idea of elaborations on the
basic indicators that you might want to keep a close eye on. They may not
necessarily be included in the formal P&L account information but some
of them could form subsidiary analyses to be used as monitoring devices
for the recovery business plan.

However, it is pretty certain that the basics outlined above will need
to be covered in some way: you *must* be able to monitor your sales, your
gross margin, your overhead costs and your resulting profits. In addition,
it cannot be stressed too many times that cash is the absolute measure
without which you are certainly doomed to fail.

The availability of information that goes to create a balance sheet is of
less immediate concern if you are keeping a close eye on stocks, debtors
and creditors as you go along, but once you have collected those you are
most of the way to creating a balance sheet, anyway. The balance sheet is
less time critical than the others, since it represents a snapshot of what
is (to be completely correct, *was*) at any given time and becomes
immediately out of date as soon as it has been compiled. But its main
value is as a check against the two other principal measures, since it
provides a datum point for cross-referencing cash and profit.

Whatever else you do in establishing your information needs, you
must insist that the preparation of timely monthly management accounts
is accorded the importance it deserves. The information that they will

provide is supplementary to the more immediate information which you will be collecting in 'flash' reports on a daily or weekly basis. But, if properly analysed, these accounts will reveal trends and patterns which will not appear anywhere else. And their single most important use is to convince the bank manager that you are making progress in turning the company around.

Profit and loss items

Turnover

In all but the simplest businesses it is important to know where your custom comes from; which parts of your business are not pulling their weight in sales; which are generating enough sales to break even and which are growing strongly. In consequence you should consider breaking turnover down by *site* (in a multiple site business if you decide to keep it so, of course) and by *product line*, as a minimum. Additional analyses might include sales by *sales area* if you sell into different geographic areas or even sales by *salesperson* if the salespeople are few enough to track without descending into too great an amount of detail.

Cost of sales and gross margin

As a minimum the cost of sales should differentiate between the cost of *raw materials* and the cost of *attributable labour* and should do so on the formal P&L account. However, a potential problem of analysis immediately arises which will complicate examination of the profitability of sales actually made by the business: this is the knotty problem of items part completed during the month.

Be very wary of accountants who want to carry forward costs of labour to items put into stock (that is, not completed by month end) at chargeout rate (the rate charged in costing jobs to customers). This artificially inflates the value of stock and consequently leads to balance sheet inflation. This then allows scope for all sorts of mischief with other working capital items and gives a massive opportunity for misleading accounts to be produced. It effectively takes an amount of profit into the balance sheet for items which have not yet been sold – and possibly never will be.

In a more robust form of accounting for this form of stock movement, all labour costs should be taken into the P&L in the month in which they are incurred and labour costs are then attributed to unfinished items at the cost to the business of employing that labour, regardless of chargeout rate. This is simple and easily understandable; it gives you the margin on what you actually managed to sell during the period for which the accounts have been compiled. You have paid for the labour, it has affected your cashflow and there is no way that you can escape its effects.

If you are accounting properly, you cannot avoid carrying labour costs forward into the balance sheet since to do otherwise would have the effect of distorting the profit and loss account adversely and would mix items in the balance sheet which do carry attributable labour (items produced for stock as a policy, part assemblies for instance, or items awaiting definite contractual sale) with those that do not. To do anything else tends to confuse a cashflow statement with a profit and loss account. (To be consistent, if you wanted to isolate the margin on only what the business actually sold during the accounting period, you would have to eliminate the value of part-completed items from turnover. This would then give rise to horrendous definitional problems which would tie up the accounts departments in knots.)

However, be aware always of the distinction between management accounts and statutory accounts. The law dictates that you have to compile statutory accounts in a certain way and the auditors will produce these for you. You are at liberty to produce your management accounts in whatever format is intelligible to you (and is suitable for your target external audiences of bank manager and other shareholders, perhaps), provided of course that you keep valid books of account. No matter what the accountants argue the statutory treatment requires (and it can change), make sure that your accounts department only includes labour at cost in your management accounts when carrying forward the value of part-completed items or subassemblies into stock.

Needless to say, the treatment accorded to cost of sales should match the analysis of turnover which you have settled upon so that you can identify the *gross margin* on each type of activity.

All other costs are effectively indirect (although again there can be disputes on the accounting definition of these items) and the treatment of them in profit and loss terms is very much up to the individual. As a minimum, they should be treated in the same way in the business's management accounting system as they were treated in the business plan – although effective cost control may demand that they be isolated further. It is also sensible to disaggregate the costs in the same way as the turnover has been broken down to allow operational parts of the business to be loaded with their correctly attributable costs. Taking all overheads into a central pool is generally not a very helpful way of analysing costs since it tends to equate apples with pears and prevents effective distinction between controllable and non-controllable costs.

There are some central overheads which cannot be sensibly split out or which require too much analysis in comparison with the worth of the information they then disclose. In my experience, costs which are entirely under the control of the central management function are best regarded as a central cost for which there is no countervailing profit inflow. Some costs you just have to regard as inescapable and un-attributable to any of the operating divisions of the business.

All these items should be set out against the original budgets that you established for them so as to give a comparison of actual figures, budget and variance. Examples of monthly sets of management information, using these principles, are given in Appendix 2.

Key points

1. The information which you need to run the business must satisfy three tests: it must be Accurate; it must be Relevant; it must be Timely.

2. You may be able to get away with just monitoring P&L account, balance sheet and cashflow at month end if your business is very simple. More likely you are going to have to review some more elaborate analysis and probably with greater frequency.

3. Think about devising a few basic measures which you look at every week – flash results – which may be crude but will give you a pointer to the way things are going. In the darkest times you should certainly watch writs and prioritise them.

4. You must never neglect the most important measure of all, your cash position, which you should review daily.

5. Don't allow yourself to be fobbed off with poor quality information that only approximates to what you want, because of a poor excuse or by a specious argument.

6. Do take the best from the existing system and use it – apart from everything else, the continuation of some familiar measures will probably boost staff morale.

7. Trim your information requirements to match the basics of monitoring the recovery plan that you have established; think simply and avoid overcomplication.

8. Unless you are sure that you have an information system that is sufficiently robust for your needs in running the business through those whom you have delegated tasks to, you may be better off retaining control yourself until such time as you do have confidence.

9. The introduction of a new management system may well throw into relief the strengths and failings of subordinate managers, in a variety of ways.

10. Financial information is not the entirety of the information which you should monitor.

Chapter 10

Dealing with the bank

We have used the aviation analogy extensively during the course of this book to help illuminate the problems and solutions that are encountered in bringing a business back to health. The analogy is particularly appropriate – even if we stretch it a little to make a point – when we begin to consider the interaction between the struggling business and its bank and suppliers.

At its root, business is combat. So, to use our analogy, it is a bit like an aerial dogfight with pilots notching up business victories instead of enemy planes, as a measure of their prowess – and in order to survive. Conducted largely in grim silence, the battle is fought above a landscape littered with the remains of earlier combats. Competitors circle round each other for much of the time seeking to score an advantage in speed of response or manoeuvrability that will allow them to shoot their competitors down in flames so they can press ahead to the target of winning more customers. The air is filled with combatants circling, wheeling and diving, all seeking an advantage over each other

Every so often a plane pitches up, a wing drops as cashflow becomes disrupted and the plane/business enters a vicious spiral as cashflow diminishes. The tightness of the spin increases as suppliers become difficult and production reduces further. The frantic pilot/manager gawps at the unresponsive controls as the situation worsens and the Red Baron – the business's banker – sensing that the situation is irrecoverable, moves in for the coup de grace . . .

And the primary reason that this comes about is because the pilot/business manager did not pay enough attention, when the troubles began, to two main enemies: the business's banker and the business's suppliers. For the truth of the situation is that, while the support of both these parties is essential if a business is to work properly, the moment that a problem is encountered they become potential enemies of the business since their interests and the business's interest will no longer necessarily coincide.

We shall deal with suppliers in the next chapter; for this chapter we shall confine our attention to bankers – most of whom are nothing like the Red Baron, of course. In truth, if you manage to get your banker on your side in trying to recover the business, that is probably worth three squadrons of Spitfires (as Adolf Galland, the German fighter commander, remarked when asked what further resources he wanted in order to win the Battle of Britain). And in recent years it has become apparent that the attitude of the major clearing banks towards businesses going through a rough patch has changed markedly in the businesses' favour. (That does not mean to say that they are any more tolerant of terminally ill businesses, though, and the moral to that is, be very careful that you know which you are involved in when you start to try to recover a business.)

Few businesses now manage to conduct their affairs without some form of temporary borrowing, usually in the form of an overdraft. And since one of the key features of a business that is entering into problems is, as we have seen, an increasing demand for cash, it is very unlikely that a business with problems will be able to avoid negotiating its future cash requirements with a bank. Either an existing overdraft has to be safeguarded for the bank, or extra cash will be required to help the business lift itself out of its problems. This means that when a business gets into trouble with its cashflow, one of the most closely interested parties to the problem will be the bank which has lent money.

As we noted above, the chances of a recovery succeeding are greatly enhanced if it has the bank manager's support. Without this, in fact, the chances of it succeeding are greatly diminished. Dealing with the clearing bank manager thus becomes an essential part of the recovery plan and because of the critical importance of the bank's attitude to both the plan and the business, it should be regarded generally as too important to be left to subordinates or to be delegated. This is one task that you should ensure that you do yourself from start to finish – into the recovery and beyond.

The reason for this is that since loans and overdrafts are usually made with some form of fixed charge over book debts or assets, the banker is potentially worst enemy and best friend of the recovery manager at one and the same time. This is because the charge over assets either gives the banker power to kill the business if the risks to recovering the loans appear to be too great for further help to be contemplated (leading the banker to seek to recover whatever can be saved out of the mess) or provides the comfort that the bank has a tangible security which will shelter the loan. How you treat your banker and how you present your case will have a substantial bearing on which way the bank chooses to view your business.

You must recognise in your dealings with the bank that you are starting off negotiations on the wrong foot, from a position of potentially overwhelming disadvantage in securing additional financial help. This is in addition to the fact that the attitude of the bank manager to the account may well change when the business gets into trouble: what was once a customer producing profit and entitled to be courted for business has now become simply a risk that may need to be written off. This is even more likely to be the case if one of the main causes has been that the management information system has been producing bad or deficient information. Not only will there be the natural reaction that problems are less pleasant to deal with than success but there may be something of a tinge of annoyance on the manager's part that they should have spotted the problem earlier themselves. Almost certainly the bank manager will face that question from superiors.

This then gives rise to a three-pronged problem for the manager of a business in trouble: dealing with the bank (and not necessarily the bank manager who faces you across a table but some faceless superior in the bank whom you have never met and will never get the chance to meet); dealing with the suppliers to keep production going; and dealing with the conflicting demands of both those parties. They both want cash to satisfy their own particular requirements and cash is in short supply. How do you make less cash go further?

The greater part of the answer is by talking to the bank manager about what you are going to do, to convince the bank that it would help itself by helping you. The key to this approach depends largely on the size of the problem that you face, since in determining what to do with an ailing business the bank faces a dilemma of its own. Its top priority at all times is risk reduction: in pursuit of this it will want to restrict its exposure by minimising the amount of money that it lends to the struggling business. But at the same time, cutting back on the availability of cash to a struggling business may precipitate the very problem the bank wishes to avoid. If the decline has arisen suddenly and the amount of money that is out on loan or overdraft is large, then you are probably in a better position to negotiate with the bank about how you are *jointly* going to overcome the problem that *both* of you face than if you have only a modest amount of debt which is fully covered in security terms by personal guarantees given by the principals in the business. For the latter is a situation where the bank faces a no-lose series of options; even if winkling the value out of a personal guarantee takes time, it is probable that the capital value of the bulk of the loan to the business will still be protected. (If you are invited by the bank to help recover the company then of course your negotiating stance over what assistance you expect to be accorded by the bank is very much different, of course.)

Since banks usually attach terms to their loans that they should receive timely management information, it is likely that the bank will be one of the first to know that problems are arising. This means that you must act fast if you want to retain the trust of the bank and engage their active support in letting you sort out the business's problems. So, almost without exception, one of the first things that you should do once you have begun to establish the basics of your recovery plan is to talk to the bank manager about your situation. This should be closely followed by a series of discussions with your critical suppliers. The tactical approach to this is dealt with in the next chapter but it is sufficient to note here that you should let all the other parties know that you are in consultation with them.

In each case you will have to temper what you tell them with a judicious examination of what they actually need to know to help you further. You must tell the truth of course – but you need not tell the *whole* truth *all the time* to *everybody*. Whatever you decide to tell suppliers and bankers about the detail of your situation, the abiding principle in your discussions should be that you will attempt at all times never to spring surprises.

This is particularly important when you are dealing with banks. All banks operate to broadly the same systems and you have to remember that in all likelihood you will be dealing with a manager who should be more properly called an account handler, given the limited amount of discretion allowed to such managers in dealing with problems of this sort by themselves and on their own initiative. This can work for you and against you, of course, but it certainly tends to make individual managers cautious and unwilling to commit themselves about how much they can help you.

Since the amount of latitude allowed to individual managers is minimal (unless you have the misfortune to be dealt with by one of the divisions that specialise in seriously awry cases) the manager you are dealing with will have to report to a superior before any course of action can be put into effect. That manager will probably have to report to another tier of authority and each of the reporting managers will be judged internally on their ability to control the losses that their lending book suffers (among other measures).

Once the account began to get into trouble, it will have become an 'exceptions case' that will need to be reported on at frequent intervals in order to comply with the bank's internal controls. This means that reports from you will be required to allow the manager to write reports to superiors. This in turn means that you will have to decide fairly early on in your recovery plan what level of information you are sensibly going to be able to give to the bank manager. As we have seen, there may be special covenants attached to loans and overdrafts which require the provision of certain information anyway. But you are entitled to argue the case that the provision of rubbish to the bank does no good to either party and is best dispensed with until you can be more certain about the quality of the information you are imparting. The bank manager should be sympathetic to this argument if one of the causes of the decline of the business is that information systems have broken down. The clincher to this line of reasoning – but be wary how you express it – is that to repeat poor information is worse than useless as far as the bank manager is concerned in reporting the case to superiors.

When you make arrangements for this first meeting with the bank manager you should ensure that you will have enough time to prepare for it. Don't make the appointment until you are happy that you can go along armed with the first draft of your recovery cashflow so that you can indicate the major elements of your recovery plan – even if they are not yet finalised in detail.

You must be prepared to outline in brief the conclusions of your first examination of the business's problems – including the difficult bits – but don't go with reams of paper analysis that you struggle to organise properly and which overwhelm the logic of your case by their sheer volume. The bank manager is looking for a strategic assessment of the situation and an indication that you know the route out of the mess. You must be incisive and decisive. Remember what has happened from the bank's point of view: suddenly this account has gone pear-shaped and it is not yet very clear why. The bank manager will probably be some steps behind you in appreciating the detail of what went wrong, so lay out where you have been in order to explain where you are and then indicate your plan for the best course for where you want to go.

Do not shrink from letting the bank manager know that it may get rougher yet, if you think it will. Remember that the worst thing that you can do to bank managers – apart from losing them their loans – is to give them nasty surprises, since that puts a black mark in their record book with their superiors.

Your initial cashflow should have shown you whether you will need help to get you out of the business's difficulties. Remember that it is no part of a banker's job to supply financial resources that the shareholders should stump up. But even so, you should flag the necessity of the business receiving additional cash at some time and, most importantly, indicate how you expect to get past any short-term cash humps while you are arranging for further shareholder support or for some other form of refinancing.

Your cashflow should not go into the details of how you intend to restrict expenditure on minor items. What the bank manager will want to know at this early stage is the strategy that you are going to adopt – the large items. So you should be concentrating on the fact that you are going to trim central overheads by about X per cent; that you are going to shut the widget division and sell all the company cars. It is that level of disaggregation that the bank is going to want to know, not how you will move to second class postage from tomorrow or only empty the waste paper bins every other night.

Your immediate case to the bank manager has, in essence, three legs. These are first, that there is cashflow which is workable with some accommodation from all sides; second, that there is time to effect a recovery based on the recovery plan that your cashflow suggests; and third, that there is more sense in having a smaller volume of decent information that can be relied upon with some degree of certainty in a difficult situation as a means to controlling the recovery, rather than in having rubbish whose validity may be highly questionable and may lead you further up the wrong path.

You must be careful in arguing these points, though, for to over-emphasise them may well rebound on you to your significant disadvantage. If you overstress the point about the poverty of the management information, you risk eliciting the knee-jerk reaction of any frightened banker – the investigating accountants' report. Ways of dealing with accountants' reports and the call for having them are considered at length in Chapter 13, since it is a stone-cold certainty that you are going to be subjected to one of these precious exercises at some point. However, for the time being, when you are finding your own feet, they are a form of diversion that you can do without if you can avoid it. If you can't, then the only thing to do is to try to limit the damage to your own plans and use of time and to make the best of the exercise that you can by ensuring your particular interests are covered in the review.

Assuming that you are able to agree these points, then you should establish together with the bank manager the following:

1. the bench-mark information that you are going to give to the bank;
2. the frequency with which you expect to be able to give it;
3. how many weeks the establishment of a good management information system is going to take.

This last point is so that so that you can say when you expect proper information to be available and therefore when you might be able to expand the basic information that you are agreeing to go forward with. Since you should have done all this for yourself very early into the exercise, in order to decide how you are going to monitor the recovery yourself, it should not be too difficult to hold out reasonable expectations for all these categories.

You should try to contain the information that you are going to give on a regular basis to the minimum sensible amount that you know you can rely on – even if for the time being that is little more than sales figures. A bank manager who has been involved with the account for any time will probably have as good an idea as anyone of the rough level of business needed to support the overheads, so may well agree that your own flash measures of performance are suitable and feel happy to accept them.

Try to negotiate a reduction in the management information required by the covenants, if there are any. Don't be frightened of asking for this: breaking the information requirement for good cause rather than negligently (or petulantly) is not a material reason for the bank to withdraw funding and a sensible manager should be willing to help you out provided that you can make a good argument that the situation is only temporary.

But beware at all times of making promises. If you do feel the need to blurt out a promise then make it a low-level one, nothing more than that you will meet again in ten days' time to report progress and certainly nothing as elaborate as that you will sort out the problems of the business in three months.

However, on those things that you do agree make religiously sure that you keep your side of the bargain. Your principal task is one of trying to establish trust with the bank manager in a situation where the bank has been let down by the performance of the business. If you can convince the bank manager that you can be relied upon for keeping your word on the small things then the bank will probably be more willing to back you when it comes to deciding on the larger ones.

In this regard, you should continue the policy that you established at the first meeting, of being completely open as far as management information is concerned. There is simply no sense in trying to conceal bad information from the bank manager. It will have to come out in the long run. And if it comes out stale you will have done yourself no good in furthering your cause with the bank. You have to meet with and deal with bad news head-on.

That does not mean that you should neglect the art of news management – since, as with everything else, presentation is all. If you know that a piece of good news about forthcoming orders will follow in a matter of hours a piece of bad news that you have now about last month's turnover, then hang on until you can report both together so that the sting is taken out of the bad news. But don't be tempted to hang on indefinitely and be careful only to compare like with like. If you try to equate the apple of turnover collapse last month with the pear of debtor recovery from 95 days to 93 days you will merely make the banker think that you can't distinguish between the important and the merely interesting – and with some justification, probably.

Your aim in all this effort should be to generate cash to remove the pressure from your balance sheet by removing pressure from day-to-day activities. A subsidiary aim – and one very much for the medium term once the recovery is well and truly established – should be to shift overdraft into some less volatile form of borrowing such as medium-term loan. The precise circumstances of the business have to be considered before you bargain for this with your clearing banker, since the bank may be willing only to shift the same amount of overdraft into loan and thereby effectively call it by another name. If it is done too early, this will leave the bank with the beneficial consequence of unaltered security and regularised payments, while leaving you with an unworkable level of free cash to meet the needs of your business. Since any shift between overdraft and loan will also leave your balance sheet gearing unaffected, it is of little real benefit to you . Your objective should be to trade the uncertainty of the overdraft for the certainty of regular repayments only after you have assured yourself that you have the working capital headroom within which to operate your business.

Key points

1. Once you have fallen into problems then you will find that the bank's interests and yours diverge.

2. You must address the problems that the bank is now facing as a matter of urgency if you are to retain their support.

3. Don't go to the bank with reams of paper analysis; take a summary and provide further information on request.

4. Do go prepared in the detail of your recovery plan.

5. Do not shrink from indicating that further help or time may be needed – better to get that out of the way now even if no offer of help is forthcoming. Show how you intend to get over any cash humps that exist.

6. Your case should have three legs: there is a good business (why?); the amount of time it will take to produce results (and the assumptions involved); and the amount of accurate management information ('MI') that you can guarantee to produce.

7. Be open with the bank manager – but don't forget the art of news management.

8. Never spring nasty surprises on the bank manager.

9. Never be tempted into making promises that you can't keep.

Chapter 11

Dealing with suppliers

Businesses that have not used formal banking arrangements to extend their cashflow may well have used informal, and unauthorised, arrangements. One of the prime sources of cash to a business in the short term is its supplier base. Some, a very few, businesses can manage to sell their own product and generate cash before they have to pay their own suppliers – which is a very useful arrangement if it can be maintained – but most businesses have to cope with a period of trade when a supplier or series of suppliers require to be paid before the customers have paid up for what they have consumed.

Complicated manufacturing businesses are the most likely to be prone to disparities between payment from customers and payments to suppliers since an extended product manufacturing time will usually result in suppliers requiring payment before payments are received from customers. This will result in a 'lumpy' cashflow with periods of cash famine followed by cash surplus. Problems in the company's performance will undoubtedly magnify these positions – pushing the company into a very unstable financing position if deeper problems are experienced.

For the recovery manager faced with an immediate cash deficit, the most obvious method of increasing cash availability is temporarily to push payments to suppliers – and other creditors – to the limit of their tolerance. This is a route which should not be overlooked as a means of overcoming a short-term problem but it has at least three drawbacks. First, least importantly, it defers the problem only for a short while since the suppliers will have to be paid at some time.

Second, of greater consequence, like all destabilising inputs to the business, it will take very much longer to recover from than the time it takes to implement. Unless the business involved has a cashflow with regular, very substantial payments which will provide occasional periods of large cash surplus when all suppliers can be brought up to date, then the extension of creditor days will take a long time to claw back since the root of the problem has not been tackled. It is probable that the cashflow problem was caused by lack of margin which manifested itself as lack of cash. Raising margin is not something that can be done overnight. Furthermore, and paradoxically, to effect a beneficial change in margin usually requires a further application of cash, either because new investment has to be made or because old resources have to be paid off as well.

Third, and most problematic, suppliers are not happy when their customers take longer to pay than they anticipated. Extension of their credit periods may well have serious knock-on effects for them, resulting in deliberate or involuntary restrictions on the availability of crucial components for future production.

Suppliers will usually become only gradually aware of the problem that is behind an increase in the time taken by the customer business to pay its bills, since they do not see the bigger picture available, say, to the bank by virtue of the bank's closer relationship and its source of direct information. What is more, as far as the individual supplier is concerned, the true position can be temporarily disguised by all sorts of other factors: increasing or decreasing levels of business with the customer, general changes in business activity, even the assiduousness or laxity with which suppliers manage their credit policies and so on.

Once the supplier does recognise the true pattern, though, their priority – if they have a debt outstanding with a struggling company – becomes one of short-term cash recovery, which can greatly increase the problems of the struggling business. The supplier's initial reaction, to recover the outstanding debt, will probably be closely followed by a restriction of the terms that were previously allowed the ailing customer until creditworthiness can once more be proved by meeting (usually) tighter credit terms over a period of time.

This has the unfortunate effect of choking supplies for future production, thereby further minimising cashflow and precipitating another vicious spiral which can lead to negative outcomes for all concerned: supplier chases customer, restricts credit levels in consequence, leading to the customer reducing their own production levels, reducing cash generation, leading to more suppliers chasing the customer and so on. The conclusion to this dance is inescapable if it is left to itself. Going back to our aviation analogy, unlike some aeroplanes, businesses will never pull out of a spin by themselves. Depending on the characteristics of the planes they are flying, pilots may be able to take their hands off the controls and expect the plane to recover; the business manager never can.

We have already seen that one of the first things that you should do once you have begun to establish the basics of your recovery plan is to talk to the bank manager about your situation. This should be closely followed by a series of discussions with your critical suppliers – of whom there should be no more than four or five if you are ruthlessly honest – to let them know edited highlights of your situation. (You should also talk to other creditors too and this is dealt with later in this chapter.) Those edited highlights will be greatly reinforced in their value if you are able to say to the individual suppliers that you have told the bank the same (general) story and that you have the support of the bank in what you are trying to do.

In each case you will have to temper what you tell individual suppliers with something of what they want to hear. And you will also have to be discriminating in your judgement of what they need to know – but the same rules apply here as apply to banks. The abiding principle in your discussions should be that you will attempt never to surprise them. It is much preferable from everybody's point of view that a realistic assessment of the situation is passed on than that a series of over-optimistic promises are made which prove to be unattainable.

As with every other aspect to the recovery plan that you put into motion, there are tactical considerations which have to be observed when dealing with suppliers. The first of these, as we have come across before, is that it is better to deal with the problem while it is small than wait until it has reached proportions which make it a crisis for everyone. The problem here, of course, is knowing exactly what is a crisis for different suppliers. Generally speaking, small suppliers who are more heavily dependent on your business will probably reach their threshold of pain before large multinational suppliers. So you might think that you can spin out the large suppliers for longer. But many large, national suppliers are organised with depot-run supply systems that are strictly controlled from the centre with no discretion allowed to the local manager. There will be little room for the local manager to give you any extra terms.

Talks with crucial component manufacturers should probably be held as an early priority since without their support you will find your plans are beached. But beware of overlooking the strategically crucial component in favour of volume suppliers, since you may find that the lack of availability of a certain part that you would not ordinarily regard as crucial holds up production, thereby worsening your cashflow. 'For the lack of a nail . . .'

Needless to say, part of this approach – of making sure that you get to the problem while it is still small enough to handle – should be to approach individual suppliers just after you have made a payment to them, while the account is still being serviced, in other words, and before it has reached the stage where a credit recovery problem has arisen. It is generally not a good idea to pay off an account completely in anticipation of a meeting going more smoothly since all that you have then done is to remove the problem entirely as far as the supplier is concerned. Bluntly, you still want them on the hook as far as future payments go but you have to judge carefully the point at which the problem becomes either too large or insufficiently large for them to worry about.

The next point to make is a corollary of the last: it is usually better for you to approach the supplier than to have them approach you with what has become a problem in their eyes. This obviously means that you must undertake a rapid appreciation of who the crucial suppliers are and their relative significance to the various parts of your business.

The first factor to be borne in mind when you are initiating negotiations with suppliers is to make sure that you talk to the correct person. This may sound too obvious to bear further examination but it is of considerable importance. You will be wasting your time if you explain your intentions to the manufacturing supervisor of your supplier only to find that you should have been talking all along to the credit controller; you may also harden the supplier's position against you since you will have alerted them prematurely to your requests. Or you will have done yourself no good at all if the only person with authority to discuss credit terms is the MD.

Meetings with suppliers are generally better conducted on their home territory, for a number of reasons. First, by going to see them at your own instigation you have taken the initiative and given yourself a psychological advantage. You have told the supplier by your actions in seeking a meeting and taking the trouble to go to see them that you want to reach a solution and that you are not letting things slide. This is an important technical advantage in reaching a compromise over the rate of payment.

Second, by going to see them at their premises you have the chance to assess their business: whether it appears busy, its overall size, the credit control arrangements and so on. This may give you a clue as to how you might pitch your terms for extended payment.

Third, by going to their premises you deny the supplier the chance of seeing how busy – or not busy – your business is. That allows you to decide what to say about the state of activity of your business. This may be a crucial factor in their decision-making, since if they reach the conclusion that your problems are temporary they will probably be willing to extend credit rather than lose a customer.

Finally (and not to be derided), if the meeting does get rough then, as visitor, you have the advantage of being able to determine when you want to leave. If the meeting is held in your office, the irate supplier can hold you to ransom by extending the meeting until you have to concede their case or be rude and ask them to leave. Since you are seeking to enlist their support, that is a poor outcome for you.

Never forget, too, wherever and under whatever conditions the meeting is being held, that you *are* a customer and if your supplier loses you they will have to find someone to replace your business. It is probably going to be in their interest to support you if they can and if you can offer them a reasonable prospect of recovering their money over a slightly more extended period than they had allowed for. To this end you should emphasise in your arguments the benefits of your continuing custom.

You should always approach the individual supplier with a definite suggestion about how you are going to overcome your mutual problems, rather than allowing the discussions to drift into a negotiation. Not only does this push the likelihood of the settlement the way that you want it to go, it also reinforces the belief on the part of the supplier that you have control of the situation in your own business. This has the effect of bolstering the small psychological advantage you have already generated by having taken the problem to the supplier rather than waiting for the problem to hit you, like a rabbit caught in the headlights of an oncoming car.

You may also decide to reduce the number of suppliers that you use as part of the process of reducing your cashflow problems. By doing this you may find it possible to defer further some of the demands of suppliers whom you have decided to eliminate from your supply list. You may also find that hints that you will have to drop suppliers unless you achieve better credit terms from them – which are in effect disguised price reductions, of course, and will therefore benefit your margin, which is what you are trying to achieve – may elicit some movement on their part. A negotiating tactic that can sometimes work in this way is to draw the supplier into a situation where they see themselves as part of both the problem and the solution. But be wary of using supplier list reduction as a sustained tactic since secondary sources of supply can be very useful when the main source dries up because of payment problems.

You will probably find yourself being pressed at some point in such negotiations to offer a revised schedule of payments to suppliers. It is difficult to avoid negotiating some sort of schedule if you want suppliers to come along with you – and having a suggestion to make is the first stage in having your proposal accepted – but the great danger here is that you will end up with a negotiated level with so many suppliers that your position overall is really no better than at the outset. Harsh though it may be, your target should be to stretch your account with as many smaller suppliers as you can, reach general accommodation with the main suppliers and confine hard agreements to a handful of critical suppliers.

What you must be certain of, though, is that if you give such commitments then you are able to honour them. It is pointless to go through the negotiations to secure agreements over different terms –

which are after all going to cost both sides money – only to throw the
result away because your planning was not up to scratch in the first place.
You must be absolutely certain that you can keep the agreements that you
have negotiated. The best way to do that is to be rock-solid certain about
the cashflows that you have constructed. The problem that you face here,
of course, is that you probably will have had to construct your cashflows
on assumptions regarding the willingness of many suppliers to enter into
the agreements you are now negotiating. If they do not all come up to the
mark or even if one crucial supplier refuses to agree to your terms, then
you risk the collapse of the whole plan. There is little that you can do
about this: acceptance of the revised terms is going to be central to your
plan's success and if you cannot achieve agreement then you will
probably have to recognise that the recovery has stalled and either try
more formal methods of reaching agreement (see Chapter 12) or accept
that the recovery is not possible at all.

There are certain tactics that can be utilised here to try to generate
compliance with your suggestions. Suppliers as a group will be reassured
by the assistance – or at least the forbearance – of the bank. They will be
very concerned that it will be the bank (which will be protected by an
array of fixed and floating charges, as they will know well from their own
experience) which will be the beneficiary of their acquiescence to your
suggestions if things go wrong. By holding discussions with the bank as a
first step you may be able to reassure them about the bank's attitude even
though you will not be able to give them any form of guarantees about the
bank's behaviour.

You may be able to suggest some forms of legal protection for them
in terms of retention of title – although this is very tricky given the powers
of the receiver, if the worst comes to the worst, and the practical effects of
legal doctrine which effectively eliminates the rights of subcomponent
manufacturers in the event of receivership (see Appendix 4).

One of the factors that many small suppliers will be also be concerned
about is that they are going to be alone in surrendering some form of
commercial advantage and then be taken for a ride while more muscular
suppliers manage to resist giving anything away.Small suppliers will be
reassured about the prospects for the long-term future of your business if
one or more of the larger suppliers have already agreed to assist by
deferring their payments.

You may achieve some success in kick-starting the process by getting
sympathetic customers to purchase direct from 'difficult' suppliers and
then have components free-issued to you. It is not always necessary to
reveal your hand entirely in this when you approach a customer for such
help – customers in particular need of your product may be willing to
help simply to expedite the manufacture of their order; the provision of
individual components on a free-issue arrangement can be 'sold' to some

customers on that basis without getting into tricky discussions about cashflow problems.

While it is important to encourage individual suppliers to co-operate with and participate in your general plan to ease your cashflow problems, you do not want them getting together to discuss between them the strategy that you have put forward. As long ago as 1776, Adam Smith, one of the first systematic observers of commerce, remarked: 'People of the same trade seldom meet together . . . but the conversation ends . . . in some contrivance to raise prices.' That observation is as accurate today as it was two hundred years ago. If you allow your suppliers to meet together or to pass information to each other about what you have offered each of them, then the initiative shifts from you to them – to your likely detriment.

It is almost certainly implicit in the cashflow that you will have constructed that you are going to concentrate the payments that you can afford in the hands of fewer suppliers. The consequence of this is that you are going to have to tough it out with some of your suppliers: the smaller ones, the weaker ones and those whose product is not crucial to your production schedules or whose goods can be substituted by other suppliers. This will mean that you are going to have to steel yourself for some rough treatment at their hands as they retaliate for the treatment they perceive themselves to be receiving at yours.

One of the most grindingly wearying features of dealing with a business in trouble is fielding the barrage of increasingly irate calls received daily from suppliers anxious to track payments for goods they supplied – and supplied in the distant past as far as their credit records are concerned. The corrosive effect that such calls can have on staff and management morale should not be underestimated. It takes considerable mental and physical stamina to deal with such calls day after day and is a task that no one can reasonably be expected to undertake over a prolonged period of time. In my experience, an undiluted three months of dealing with such calls will sap the energy of the most ebullient person and is really the longest that most people can be expected to put up with. (There are exceptions, of course: some people thrive on adversity of this type and have the necessary placidity to deal with calls while remaining calm and unflustered. But such people are exceptional.) On the basis of that three month limit some of your suppliers may be facing credit terms to you of something like 75–90 days and beyond this period of time you are almost certain to find yourself on the wrong end of County Court or High Court writs.

The first writ that you receive is the the worst one that you will have to deal with. Unless you are completely unfazed by the predicament you find yourself in, it is an unpleasant feeling to be suddenly confronted with the weight of the legal machinery that can be arrayed against you.

However, unpleasant though it is, the receipt of a writ is not the end of the world and has to be regarded as one more obstacle that has to be climbed over if you are to reach your goal.

The first writ is also unlikely to be the last one that you will receive. When they do start coming they come in clutches and you must establish a diary system so that you know when the time in which they have to be dealt with comes close to expiry. High Court writs and County Court writs have different expiry periods before they have to be settled so be careful to distinguish between them in your diary system. Since all writs are accompanied by a charge for the costs incurred in issuing the writs there is no benefit to be gained by settling a writ early and they should be left to run their course, unless there is some special reason involved – such as unblocking an otherwise closed source of supply. Be sure that you tell your bank manager about the receipt of writs and how you intend to deal with them: bank intelligence departments scan local papers to register County Court judgments (CCJs) and High Court judgments against customer companies in trouble and it is wise to let the manager know before the event rather than have the bank catch up through its own internal processes.

Many suppliers now pass the treatment of delinquent customer accounts to firms of solicitors that make a minor specialisation out of debt-chasing. You can usually buy yourself some time, *in extremis*, by making a partial payment to these firms – if you cannot find the whole amount – to stave off the hearing. If you want to play it really close to the wire then you can go to the hearing and make an offer to pay there. But that requires *very* strong nerves or a *really* tight cashflow. My advice would be to pay the writ off before it arrives in court and save yourself the humiliation of appearing before a judge, never a pleasant experience for an ordinarily law-abiding citizen.

It is wise to distinguish in your diary of writs between those initiated by the suppliers themselves, those initiated by debt collectors and those initiated by factoring companies or finance houses. You will find that it may be possible to negotiate part-payment terms even after the writs have been issued with the first category; that it is difficult to get away with anything other than majority payments with the second, and that you have to pay up completely with the last category.

Finance houses have effectively bought your debt from their clients and they have no further interest in retaining you as a customer. This is in sharp comparison, of course, to a supplier who finds there is no option but to go to law to encourage you to pay up. The fact that there is no supplier being upset might encourage you to think that you can get away with relegating the finance house to the low-priority payments list. What you must bear in mind is that suppliers will be restricted by the terms of their agreements with finance houses from using future debts to you in their credit arrangements with finance house, and also that if you fail to pay up there will be adverse consequences when you try to rearrange lines of credit for yourself in the future. Credit reference agencies, to which all the finance houses subscribe, log all writs issued to companies for non-payment of debts and the historical records kept on bad risk companies are as extensive as you would expect for a multibillion pound industry.

You are going to have to make some very hard choices about whom to pay if you try to conserve the cash you need to keep your own business alive. But pick your enemies carefully.

After they have given one warning, or at most two, most finance houses will proceed to law as a matter of course. Finance houses give no quarter in pursuing debts since they have a reputation to maintain. Once you have taken the statutory period between the issue of the writ and the date for it to be responded to, you can expect no sympathy from the finance house.

In comparison with finance houses, other creditors vary in their resolve to ensure their payment terms are observed. The landlord – who occupies a special place in the law of receiverships – may well be amenable to negotiate about rental payments and levels rather than have a property stand empty as a result of insisting on payment according to the letter of the rental agreement. Comparatively recent changes in legislation which now restrict a landlord's rights to go back to previous tenants who have assigned tenancies, in order to recover unpaid rent, weaken the landlord's position considerably and should encourage greater commerciality. Small landlords may well react differently from large property institutions, and premises on the wrong side of town are probably easier to negotiate over than prime city centre sites.

It used to be the case that the two most intransigent creditors to run up against were the Customs and Excise and the Inland Revenue. In recent years their attitude has changed markedly since they now appreciate that pushing too hard may well end in simply increasing the unemployment register. They are still far from being soft touches and the ardour with which they pursue debt will vary from region to region. But they now exercise more commerciality in their thinking than they used to. The bad publicity occasioned by pushing companies into receivership has had something of an effect. Both agencies now have regional debt management units who are amenable to discussions about how taxes can be deferred over modest periods, sometimes without any interest penalties if the system is not being abused and the case can be proven.

As with every other creditor – and more than ever with these two – tackle the problem while it is small. In addition, the Inland Revenue and Customs and Excise appreciate being told what is happening before the event rather than after it and you have nothing to lose by making a clean breast of the situation as early as you can. Furthermore you can – and should – be as open as you like in discussing your situation with both the Revenue and the Excise since the advice about collusion with other suppliers does not apply. However, be very careful to tell them both the same story since sophisticated information sharing between revenue-collecting departments of government is now the rule and the details of your case will be compared if, for instance, you make payments to one and not to the other.

Paradoxically, local authorities are often less easy to deal with unless there is a substantial employment problem in their area, even though foregoing direct cash collection is less expensive to them than it appears to be because of the quirky way that the rate support system operates. They are often so hard up for cash that they are very reluctant to forego or defer revenue.

However, it is also fair to say that their collection records and systems are often sleepy and an involuntary period of deferment can be obtained from them simply by not paying and waiting until they wake up to the fact that they are missing a payment. Remember – every penny that you can keep in your business's account for longer than it would otherwise stay is one penny closer to your goal of achieving the recovery plan.

Key points

1. As with all other aspects of managing a sick business, keep your individual problems small by dealing with them before they become big problems.

2. Keep talking to the bank manager regularly with information about what you are doing.

3. Keep talking to the critical suppliers as a matter of priority – hiding yourself away is likely to irritate suppliers who feel that they have sufficient trading importance to warrant an explanation from the person in charge. Conversely, although it may be brutal, educate your own staff to protect you from dealing with every supplier who wants to complain about late payment.

4. Try to avoid making any commitment to paying a supplier unless you know that you can keep it. In this respect, *although it is strictly against the letter of the law*, you should pick carefully those suppliers whom you pay regularly or more promptly than others.

5. When writs come in, make sure that they are assigned a correct time priority; take advantage of all the time that the legal process allows

you in scheduling payments to settle writs but do not abuse the system.

6. Make sure that you honour absolutely any obligations to the Customs and Excise and Inland Revenue when you enter into deferred payment arrangements with them.

Chapter 12

Crash landings

Any landing you walk away from is a good landing
GEORGES GUYNEMER (1894–1917),
FIRST WORLD WAR FRENCH AIR ACE

There are some situations in which no matter what you do or how hard you try you will not be able to save the business. Either the situation is too far gone or quite simply luck is not with you. The language of business and the language of aviation coincide brutally in these circumstances: you are going to crash.

But you should remember that there are two types of crashes: survivable ones and unsurvivable ones. Some crashes are obviously fatal. Everyone dies and everything goes up in smoke. However, some crashes you can walk away from – and any landing you walk away from, some would regard as a good landing! Damage may be sustained; there may be some injuries; it may take time and money to repair the effects of the crash; but the aircraft – or the business – may fly again, sometimes even with the same crew.

On the occasions when it looks as though there is no way down for a business in trouble other than to crash, there are two things to hold uppermost in your appreciation of the situation:

1. the impact of the crash can be cushioned, to some extent, for all those connected with the business if appropriate and timely steps are taken; and
2. controlling the crash can salvage a great deal from the business for shareholders, employees, customers and suppliers.

This is provided that action is taken speedily to deal with the problem. The need to move quickly is one of the themes that runs through the advice in this book but there is probably no greater urgency than at the time when a crash landing is being considered.

You should already have tried to stretch creditors, by negotiating with them, and shorten debtors as a method of generating cash for the business. The amount of success that you have had with this approach has probably not been adequate if you are now having to contemplate the imminent demise of the business. But there is a further twist to this process which can be applied to try to salvage the basic business, to give it a breathing space so that it can recover and to make the crash a survivable one.

The Creditors Voluntary Arrangement is a private arrangement between the company and its creditors which gives the company time to reorganise its finances; possibly to make a partial payment to its creditors in settlement of the debts it owes them; possibly to pay them all that it owes over a longer period of time than it would otherwise be allowed to take. Crucially, it leaves the shareholding structure, the board of the company and the secured creditors in place. All other methods of rescuing a company will disturb these to a greater or lesser degree.

There are no set rules governing what happens to payments and timings – the arrangements are completely flexible and provided that they are agreeable to over 75 per cent of the unsecured creditors present or present by proxy at the creditors meeting , they bind all creditors who were originally notified of the intention of the company to try to enter into a CVA (although secured and preferential creditors have to be in agreement with the proposals, too, as we shall see later).

The CVA requires the appointment and participation of a supervisor (called a nominee until the process is approved by creditors), who may play no direct part in the running of the business after being called in. This is unlike a receivership, where the receiver is in control of the company. The supervisor, who must be a licensed insolvency practitioner, is responsible for making sure that creditors are paid in the way that the company has agreed. This necessarily entails the supervisor being assured that the basic scheme is practicable, which usually means being instrumental in the preparation of the business plan that the company puts forward to its creditors to secure their agreement to the CVA in the first place. Once the CVA is approved, the supervisor may look after the interests of the stakeholders in the business in an active way by attending board meetings or helping to resolve problems that crop up in running the business.

This will incur a fee for assisting in the preparation of the case to go to the creditors; and there will also be charges for supervising the trust fund that is used to pay creditors the 'dividend' on the book value of their debts. This dividend is the amount that they have agreed will settle their claims against the company over the period of the CVA. These fees are likely to run in the order of £5,000 to £10,000 for setting the scheme up, with fees of perhaps of a minimum of £2,500 to £5,000 per quarter depending on the degree of active supervision thereafter.

Inevitably, the preparation of this plan to be put forward to creditors takes time if it is to be done properly. And since the creditors will be being asked to give up some of what they currently consider is due to them, it is vitally important that it be done properly and is made as attractive to them as possible in comparison with the alternatives. When they have to consider what they are going to get through supporting the CVA against what they are going to lose if they let the company go down, they will have to weigh on the one hand the benefit of having a continuing customer as well as the relief from corporation tax and VAT that they will get on their bad debts against on the other hand the cost of profit and cash foregone and administrative time spent in recording the arrangements.

Taking tax relief into account, the dividend will generally be unattractive if it is pitched at much less than 30–40p in the pound and unless it is repaid over a fairly short period of time – say, not more than six months. This level of dividend will allow most businesses to get back the cash that they actually expended in producing the goods they have supplied. Any longer than six months and the poundage has to be increased fairly stiffly if the deal is to be attractive, since interest costs will begin to bite as a factor in determining the cost of the arrangement for the creditor.

There will usually be only one chance of ensuring the co-operation of the creditors and an offer which is insufficiently attractive to them will not secure their agreement. However, it may be sensible to discuss the proposals that you are going to put forward to all creditors informally and confidentially with one or two of the senior ones. This will sound out their likely reactions to your suggestions and may help you to gauge the likely response of all the creditors. You can then pitch your proposals to all the creditors at a level which you know will be acceptable. The nominee supervisor may wish to be involved in this process – and this may give your discussions with one or two of the most significant creditors some added weight, in that they will know that the situation is being taken seriously by all concerned and that proper help is being brought to bear.

The nominee supervisor will want to check the recovery plan for its soundness under a variety of critical assumptions – turnover changes, margin changes, overhead changes and so on – before being sufficiently comfortable with it to recommend that it be put to creditors. This may take a greater or lesser amount of time depending upon the degree of diligence with which the basic plan was prepared by management in the first place; the complexity of the business; the transparency of the assumptions used; the amount of work that can be predicted for the future from either the fullness of the order book or past trading records.

Once the plan is ready – after discreet soundings have taken place with one or two creditors, perhaps – it is sent out to all the creditors with a notice convening a meeting. Great care must be taken in ensuring that *all* creditors are circulated since any who do not receive notice of the meeting are not bound by any decisions taken at the meeting and can reduce the CVA to ashes by continuing to press for payment. Any creditors who receive notice but do not choose to attend are still bound by the decisions taken at the meeting.

Secured creditors – those who have some form of charge over the business – and preferential creditors, such as Customs and Excise, Inland Revenue and the Benefits Agency, are also entitled to vote at these meetings and are required to give their approval to the process if it is to go ahead. Nothing in the plans agreed between the company and the unsecured creditors can overturn the preferential nature of these creditors, who must have their debts paid out in full before any dividend can be paid to unsecured creditors. (Although technically it is possible for the preferential creditors to agree to be paid a proportion of their debts, in practice this never happens.)

At the meeting, which will be run by the nominee supervisor, creditors will be asked to identify themselves and agree the level of the money owed to them by the company. Questions can be asked about the proposals – which the supervisor will either answer personally or direct to one of the management – and then the matter is put to a vote. In order for the scheme to work, in excess of 75 per cent by value of the creditors have to agree to accept the conditions of the scheme. If they do, then the arrangement becomes binding on *all* creditors, present or not, who have received notification.

If the agreement of the creditors is forthcoming, the agreement is then taken to the High Court for recording. (You will not be surprised to learn that this also costs money). Once this is done – and there are only technical reasons why it should not be – the agreement has the force of a legal contract between the parties and cannot be broken without penalties. As we noted above, even creditors who voted against are now bound by the terms of the agreement, as are those who did not turn up to the meeting but who were notified.

Although the business is not controlled by the supervisor once the CVA is in place, the supervisor is still responsible to the court and the creditors for its successful operation. Because of this the supervisor will want to ensure that the business is being run properly and so will require regular, frequent meetings with the management, especially during the early course of the CVA (all of which will cost money!). However, the arrangement remains (technically) a private arrangement between the company and its creditors: there is, for instance, no requirement for there to be an identification on the company's letterhead that it is in a CVA as there is with a receivership while the receiver trades on.

The plan which was put to creditors will have identified the amounts of cash that the company is expected to generate surplus to its operational requirements. These sums will be put into a trust account, with the supervisor as trustee, and used to pay the dividends to creditors. The dividends will be so many pennies in the pound of each debt payable to all creditors uniformly. Every creditor will receive the same poundage dividend at the same time.

It is almost certainly the case that there will need to be some adjustment to trading terms with suppliers who are also creditors under the CVA to reflect the fact that they are receiving repayment of past debts much more slowly than they had anticipated. It is quite common to find that companies in a CVA have to make payments in advance to suppliers – perhaps only partial payments, admittedly – but this will all have been agreed at the time that the CVA was accepted. Even so, it will impose its own problems on production scheduling, availability of crucial components and payment contingencies.

It should be evident from this that the CVA is an attractive means of rescuing the company from the brink of disaster but it is not to be seen as a soft option.

One step beyond the CVA is administration. Unlike the CVA the administrator controls the business and ensures that it runs for the benefit of creditors. This is a court-arranged affair with administrators being responsible to the court for their conduct and personally liable for some of the debts of businesses once they have taken them over. It is not a procedure to be undertaken lightly and is really designed for a company with a more fundamental problem, but which is still facing a basically profitable market-place, than the company contemplating a CVA. It might be chosen in preference to a CVA, for instance, if the nominee feels unable to support the incumbent management (as an administrator the nominee can make changes); or if there is a problem in achieving a 75 per cent majority of creditors; or if there are substantial overseas interests. Since the administrators are officers of the court, they are recognised as having authority by foreign jurisdictions (whereas a supervisor in a CVA is not).

The difference between the two could be distilled to this: the CVA is to be used to get a company over a hump of cashflow which it needs some time to sort out. The purpose of an administration is basically the same but with the overlay of a more difficult background: an attempt to salvage a business for the creditors – perhaps the employees, too, and to a lesser extent the shareholders – when the shareholders have exhausted their ability to fund it further. Usually, there is still a potentially valuable business, say because of a strong order book which can perhaps be run out over a period of time, which will generate more cash to enable more orders to be won so that the business's value can be salvaged by a sale or recapitalisation in due course. Unlike the CVA – and as in all other forms of receivership or liquidation – the administrator will be required to submit a report to the Department of Trade on the conduct of the directors prior to being appointed, to enable the regulators to determine if further action needs to be considered concerning their suitability to be directors of companies in the future.

The rules governing administration are complex and detailed since the process is not the same as the private arrangement of the CVA. Administration is not something that can be done on a DIY basis and, as we have seen, must be a conducted by a properly qualified individual who operates under the authority and responsibility of the High Court.

A competent insolvency practitioner called in to advise about a CVA would be best able to judge whether the situation is sufficiently serious to warrant the institution of an administration. It is a valid alternative to receivership since the business is salvaged for some of those who participated in it, but there will almost certainly be casualties – usually among the shareholders. Administration can just about be classified as a crash landing in our terms, but only just.

Key points

1. It should become apparent to you reasonably early in the attempted recovery whether you will have the support of your crucial suppliers; if it does not seem possible to make your available cash meet your requirements for supplier payments, consider the implementation of a Creditors Voluntary Arrangement.

2. You must move fast to utilise the limited time that is still available to you before cash runs out.

3. Prepare a cashflow plan to take to the insolvency practitioner, showing realistically what you expect to be the likely cashflow and how you expect to overcome the problem eventually.

4. Make sure that you continue to talk to crucial suppliers and gently introduce the likelihood of the CVA to them – they are likely to salvage more out of the situation in a CVA than they will if they panic now.

5. The detail of the exercise will be controlled by the insolvency practitioner who has agreed to take on your case, but you will remain in control of the commercial side of the business until all creditors are paid off the agreed poundage; at that point total control of all aspects of the operation of the business reverts to you.

Chapter 13

Accountants' investigations and after

Sooner or later in trying to recover a company, you are going to be faced with a request from your bank that a firm of accountants comes into the business to check either the validity of your systems or, more likely, the forecast information that you prepared for the bank or the value of their security. This is as certain as night follows day. It comes about because bankers are naturally cautious and would prefer to have someone else involved in the decision about whether to continue to extend overdraft facilities rather than make the decision entirely on their own.

Since you – or the company you are looking after – will be paying for this exercise, it is a costless affair for the bankers and one which they will consequently order up with abandon. Because of this, the accountants' investigation needs to be treated with caution by you, both in terms of the costs that it imposes on your business and the potential effect that it can have, in a number of ways.

There are essentially three purposes to which an accountants' investigation can be put:

1. to reinforce the pre-existing prejudices of the banker about the business – to confirm their beliefs, either way, about helping you out of the hole you find yourself in;
2. to be used as a substitute for original decision-making by the banker;
3. to act as a reconnaissance for a receivership on the part of the accountants.

This last is a particularly pernicious use of the exercise and one which, in my experience, occurs far more frequently than might be thought. Never forget that firms of accountants are in business to make money and are alive to every opportunity to do so. Every lame duck is a potential receivership case as far as some investigating accountants are concerned.

Despite their protestations, they are not there to help you – they are there to trip you up if they can and to win more work from the bank which appointed them. Remember too that they are also keen to protect their stupendously high professional indemnity insurance premiums. They don't want to make these any worse by being sued by a bank for wrong advice and the easiest advice to give to a bank with a wobbly loan is to pull it in as soon as possible.

It has to be said at the outset that it takes no great genius to find something wrong with the financial administration of a company in trouble – and it is an even easier task to cast doubt on financial forecasts prepared by a harassed management which has a primary assumption that the bank will hang on just that *little* bit longer. The investigating accountants' task in condemning a company is therefore an easy one if they wish it to be: finding ways to say no more money is usually quite simple. If you are unlucky enough to be saddled with this sort of accountant – and you will probably be able to ascertain their attitude fairly quickly into the exercise – there is little that you can do in the first instance other than prepare your case very strongly for the review meeting that you will have with the banker to discuss the report. We shall consider this below.

But as with everything else, adequate preparation for an investigation will lead to the best outcome.

We have already noted that the cost of the exercise will be down to the company to pay, and this is money that you can ill afford to spend if you are already in a tight corner. So there are a number of points to cover if you are not to find yourself spending money on a wasted exercise that will consume time and money purposelessly – and possibly harmfully to your continued ability to trade.

First of all, it is always worth checking your banking agreement to see if the bank is actually allowed to pass on the cost to you of such an exercise. It is very unlikely that the terms letter which the bank sends out will have missed this out but mistakes do sometimes happen and you could use such an omission to your benefit – not to refuse to have an investigation, but to use as a lever to prise out concessions in your favour. But you will have to bear in mind, if you do decide to press the point and you are operating on overdraft, that such money is at call and can be withdrawn at twenty-four hours' notice. It would be unwise to tweak the tail of the bank too hard in those circumstances.

You are very unlikely to get away with a flat refusal to accept an investigation but you may be able to influence it to make the situation less fraught than it would otherwise be. (It is also worth checking, while you have the banking agreement out, the nature of the security which the bank has to support the loan/overdraft. The circumstances in which banks are allowed to use the matrimonial home of a guarantor as security has been very severely circumscribed by the courts. Most banks are alive to this and have refreshed vulnerable guarantees with new ones with the requirement that the new guarantees be offered only after separate legal advice has been taken by both the guarantor and the spouse. But if you have been unfortunate enough to have had to secure an overdraft with a personal guarantee backed up with your house, it may be possible that it is of the old type and not legally watertight as far as the bank is concerned. This is not going to help you very much with the investigation itself but it is a point worth remembering for the future.)

Assuming, then, that you accept that there is going to be an investigation, the first point to remember is that *you are paying* so that that gives you certain rights and privileges. In particular, you do not have to accept the first accountant the bank comes up with to conduct the investigation: perhaps a partner in a firm to which they owe favours or with which they particularly like working. (That may also mean, of course, that the bank trusts the investigating accountant's judgement because it *is* good and that may be beneficial to you.) You will have to judge whether standing up for yourself now and refusing the initial nomination (if you believe the accountant to be a dud) is worth the possible risk of antagonising the bank manager in the longer run – and that is something that only you can judge according to the lights of your case.

Ask for an early meeting with the investigating partner – and make sure that you see a partner, not a manager – to determine the scope of the investigation that is going to be conducted. Find out how long the exercise is going to take, both so you can allow for the disruption that it is going to cause and also to judge the reasonableness of the fee that is being charged.

Consult quickly with your own auditors – who will not be eligible to conduct the investigation, by the way, since they will have an inescapable conflict of interest – to see if the proposed investigator has a particular name for being reasonable or difficult. If after talking the position over with them, you do not like the reputation of the partner who has been nominated by the bank there is no reason – *since you are paying* – why you should have that person imposed on you. But you should be ready to propose a neutral and acceptable alternative, possibly a partner of the same firm but from a different office. And you must be prepared to give a valid reason for your objection. Appearing to be petulant and having no alternative to offer will not help your case.

Once you have agreed with the bank who is going to do the work, you should ask to agree the terms of reference of the investigation with them. The reason for doing this is to help the investigation go through more smoothly and to understand what is going to be done so that you can brief your own staff. Again, don't try to delay the process by posing unreasonable objections – it won't work and will only exasperate the bank – but make suggestions or ask questions constructively and purposefully. You may even choose to incorporate into the instructions to the investigator some additional remit for your own purposes which will help both you and the bank in reaching a more rounded conclusion about the situation.

Whatever else you agree, these terms *must* include clauses to the effect that you have the right to adequate time to study the report before it is delivered to the bank – include at least a day – and that you have the right to have a supplementary report submitted, *simultaneously with the main one*, which will highlight any points on which you and the investigating accountant cannot reach agreement. You must be prepared to stand on this point when it comes to the test. Do not let the accountants bully you into letting them submit their report without these clauses being honoured and if they do, register in writing immediately what they have done with the bank manager and copy the letter to the accountants.

Most importantly, while you are discussing the terms of reference make sure that you agree a maximum cost to the exercise, to include expenses and VAT, so that you know how much of a bill you are going to face and can budget accordingly, and so that the exercise cannot turn out to be a fishing expedition conducted at your expense.

During the course of the investigation there are a number of fairly simple points which will minimise the disruption of the exercise and maximise the utility of it to you. First, make sure that the investigator has access to all the information they require quickly and efficiently. This will create a good impression as to the effectiveness of the company's administration and will minimise wasted time. This is also where time spent in discussing the scope of the investigation at the outset will begin to pay off since you will know the areas that the investigator wants to look at far better than you could have deduced from a bald letter stating simple terms – and don't forget that the bank will have discussed the situation with the investigator at length before drafting those terms.

Second, make sure that the information is up to date. Poor performance on this score will leave the investigator wondering whether you know what you are doing and will raise doubt about all the assumptions of your forecasts.

Third, make sure that everyone on your side tells the same story – and not least that they speak to the same forecast. By this time anyway you should have fixed on and be working to one forecast. Switching to another forecast midway into the accountants' report is the surest way to make everybody nervous and virtually guarantees a report which will be adverse to your best interests.

All this advice about taking control of the exercise yourself does not mean that you have to be in every discussion like some dark, baleful vulture sitting on the shoulder of your subordinates. But it does mean that everyone should have been fully briefed as to the purpose of the exercise and the need to be aware of its significance for their own individual futures. Not least, given the likely adverse effects on suppliers' confidence of learning that investigating accountants have been appointed (and the inevitable conclusions that are drawn) you must brief your staff about the need to employ appropriate discretion about the exercise.

Make sure that you attend any meetings with the investigating accountants at which the report's first draft is reviewed. Do not leave the task to a subordinate, no matter how trusted an ally; an incumbent finance director from the time that the business got into trouble will probably not be up to this on their own, for instance. Bear in mind, too, that the wrong emphasis may be placed on a crucial paragraph by someone not as alive to the seriousness and subtleties of the situation as you are. Or a crucial exposure of a fact or failing that you wished to bring into sharp focus may be hidden by someone's innocent – or otherwise – redrafting.

When it comes to paying for the report, the bank and the accountants will undoubtedly want to debit your account direct with the cost of the exercise. You should resist this and accept only that the bill will have to be paid within a certain reasonable period of time. You do not want to be put in jeopardy of having your overdraft called because you breach your covenants or limits – or more likely have to defer payment to a crucial supplier – simply because you are faced with a bill for an investigation.

Above all, refuse to accept any undertaking that the bank has the irrevocable power to dock the cost of the exercise from your account if you have not settled with the accountants over the cost of the exercise because you remain in dispute over some of the findings. Apart from the fact that the legal basis for the bank wanting the right to make such a payment is very shaky, you want to retain the power to impose the sanction of not paying for work that you might consider to be flawed and possibly negligent. The accountant is just another creditor, and should take a place at the back of the queue; and since you would not pay a plumber for badly executed work why should you pay a bad accountant?

Lastly, if all this preparation fails and you are faced with a report that you believe wrongly condemns you, you must be prepared to stand your corner and fight your case with practical evidence that the investigating accountant has got it wrong. And believe me they do – more often than not, probably, in terms of the detail – which is why their professional indemnity insurance costs are so high.

The best way to do this is to make sure that you are prepared to take your case fully documented to the regional manager of the bank if you cannot reach agreement with the local manager. You can demand to go to that level if you want to and the regional manager should agree to be available; don't be put off by suggestions from the local manager that you have gone as far up the organisational tree as you can. Put your requirements firmly, but without aggravating what is an already difficult situation. And remember that you have to be prepared with a case that is provable – and provable as to *substance* not simply as to *form*. In other words, if the accountants' report is correct in fact and in conclusion, you are probably going to get short shrift if you say that the bank should not call in its loan simply because they did not give you the twenty-four hours' notice to consider the report that was written into the agreement.

If the bank decides to accept the accountants' opinion despite your entreaties, you should prepare yourself for a difficult time in managing the business's finances. You will probably find that the next step will be for the bank to reduce the facilities available to you in order to reduce absolutely the amount of money that they have at risk. If you are within your overdraft level at the time of the investigation and report, this may mean that the level of future headroom available to you is reduced. If you are at the top of the agreed overdraft, you may find yourself having to pay money back. This will usually be done by the bank appropriating the money to its own account as it comes into yours so that you do not have the benefit of an inflow to pay suppliers or existing creditors.

Fairly obviously, this will make your task in the future management of the recovery very difficult indeed. You should probably consider very seriously at this point the introduction of a CVA (see Chapter 12) to make the best use of the time and money left to you in trying to salvage the company.

If you have been able to convince the bank that there is sufficient error in some of the report to cast doubt on the crucial parts of the rest – and it does happen – then you will probably find that you are subject to the further oversight of the intensive care department for a continuing period (usually left indeterminate as to timing and measured by the attainment of an undefined level of comfort for the bank) and that you are also asked to submit more and better management information. You may also find that the bank will require yet another investigation in due course, at more cost of course, to prove that you are recovering as you claimed you could.

If this does happen, then you should make sure that you emphasise – perhaps privately and without heat – that you require at the very least the employment of a different partner from a different office of the original investigating accountants to conduct the next investigation.

You should also strongly resist at this point the imposition of charges for the accountants' report and refuse to knuckle under immediately to the bank's probably increasingly agitated requests that the investigating accountants be paid. If the report was not accepted as to its conclusions, why should you pay for it? But in refusing to pay, bear in mind that you have to depend on the bank for some little time yet so it would be wise to be open to some form of compromise to save face – hard though that may be for you to swallow, both financially and philosophically.

Convincing the bank to set aside the report means that you can get back to instituting your recovery plan. But remember, despite the temporary significance of the effort that has had to be expended, it is only one sideshow skirmish that you have prevailed in. The battle itself has yet to be won.

Key points

1. You must prepare thoroughly for an accountants' investigation and not leave the conduct of the exercise to chance. Brief your own staff about what is going on so that appropriate help can be given to the investigators and so that the scope for rumours is minimised.

2. Don't try to fight the decision – the bank holds the trump cards – and you may precipitate a worse situation by appearing to be petulant and unreasonable.

3. Try to use the event constructively: you may learn more about the business by engaging the help of the professionals rather than by resisting the scrutiny of outsiders . . . especially since you are paying for it.

4. Find out what the investigating accountant is going to look at and make sure that you have available all the information needed, so as to minimise the disruption, time and cost of the exercise.

5. Never try to adjust forecasts during the process of an investigation; if it is evident that changes have to be made because the investigation throws up new considerations, collaborate with the accountants if at all possible to produce a new agreed plan that can be jointly presented to the bank.

6. If you disagree with the report prepared by the accountants then challenge it. But you must be prepared to challenge on substance and not simply on form.

Chapter 14

The crew

A corporate recovery is never the work of one person alone. Although direction may be given by one person – as I hope we have demonstrated, there can only ever be one pilot-in-command – the *combined* efforts of all those engaged in the operation of the business are required if the recovery is to succeed.

From this it follows that a recovery is about carrying freight and not passengers. There is no room on board the recovery aeroplane for those who cannot or will not pull their weight. To have them stay on board will increase the difficulty of the task of recovery for all the others who are contributing to the effort. And from this it follows that there are two tasks here for the recovery manager, one of which is obvious and which we have touched on before in several chapters, and one of which is, perhaps, less obvious.

As the person charged with the recovery you have to be very sure that the managers are all up to the task if the recovery is to succeed. You will probably have inherited a senior management team from what has gone before and must start to work on the recovery (largely) with what you are given. But one of the tasks that you should be certain to accomplish as soon as you can is to review the suitability of the staff in the business to make sure that they are fit for the jobs they have to perform. At several points in previous chapters we have identified points where such reviews ought to be carried out. The importance of these exercises to the satisfactory pursuit of the recovery cannot be over-emphasised. Failure to complete them and then to act upon the results will jeopardise the recovery and all the jobs of all the people in the business.

As time goes on you should also review the capabilities of the next tier of managers down – if the business is reasonably compact – or make sure that your fellow managers also undertake effective and thorough reviews of their departments, using an agreed set of criteria universally and fairly applied, and then take action on the results. Again, throughout the chapters dealing with the process of extending the recovery, we have identified points and procedures to ensure that this is done. Performing these reviews of staff to be continually sure that the abilities of the people who hold positions of responsibility match the requirements of their tasks is the first and obvious element of the long-term management of the recovery.

The second element is less obvious and one that is easily neglected, either because it is never recognised or because it is quite simply over-looked: this is the importance of the maintenance of good morale among the staff who are going to help the business survive.

Lifting morale off the floor and then propping it up until there is tangible evidence of recovery is a prime factor in a recovery once the basic plan has been established. People who are reasonably happily employed and are not worrying about whether they will still be employed at the end of the month, or about how they are going to pay the mortgage if they lose their jobs, or about whether they can find another job locally or with equivalent pay, can devote their full attention to doing their jobs. It is blindingly obvious that people with only half their minds on their jobs and the other half filled with personal concerns will perform less satisfactorily than those who can devote substantially all their attention to their jobs without distraction.

That less than satisfactory performance will translate into missed sales targets, debtors not pursued, cashflow misfiring and sloppy production. Any one of those can be a killer – and in some combination they are what contributed to bringing the business low in the first place. Your job – and what you have worked so hard at so far – is to eradicate those poisons from the body of the business, to prevent slipping past you a (sometimes seemingly minor) component of the recovery process that will produce the effect of the company sliding back into its bad old ways through poor execution of the plan you have developed.

Unfortunately, when your own optimism is under constant attack it is sometimes very difficult to appreciate that others need boosting too. This brings us to another aspect of the job of the recovery manager: the maintenance of your own morale. Since the recovery process is usually a long and arduous one, with constant, difficult decision-making and an uncommon amount of personal application to a task that can be very wearing, some managers find that there is a need to have someone outside the business with whom they can consult about their plans to reduce the mental attrition that the process can bring about. Using someone outside the business as a sounding board can be a very useful way of reducing the amount of pressure that inevitably builds up when a task is tackled single-handedly. Sometimes wives or husbands can help; sometimes auditors or other professional colleagues. But it is wise to try to pick someone sympathetic to what you are doing, even if they are only passingly familiar with the type of business that you are engaged in. The simple act of having to explain the basis of your decisions to an outsider will probably greatly help the clarity of your decision-making as well as giving you pause for reflection on the wisdom or appropriateness of the particular paths that you think you are about to choose.

But to return to our main thrust, if widespread good morale is such a crucial component of the recovery process, how do you go about reviving it, boosting it and maintaining it? The truth is that there is no easy answer. Most of the other aspects of the recovery dealt with in this book are observances of obvious good practice that can be applied to various parts of the problem in a technical fashion: if you know the principles of what you are going to do, then you can execute the action and, further-more, you will probably get better at it as you practise it more. Cashflows become easier to do with practice; evaluating the capabilities of indi-viduals becomes an easier task with repetition; knowing where to start with a multifaceted problem becomes easier once you have mastered the basic analytical technique. But demonstrating leadership – which is what we are really talking about now – is not something that can be taught in quite the same way. And since there will be widely differing views among individuals about what constitutes good leadership, it is a very difficult thing to pin down.

Most people recognise good leadership when they see it or read about it but isolating its components is a difficult task. As a result, unfor-tunately for what is probably one of the most significant considerations of the arguments advanced in this book, there is very little concrete advice that can be laid down, other perhaps than to study the way that someone you think is a good leader goes about their task and then to try to emulate the way that they do it.

But whatever you choose to do, remember the guiding rule – there can be only one pilot-in-command. Leadership at its root is probably simply making or being willing to make decisions that others would rather leave to somebody else. Remember, too, that if you do not choose to exercise leadership, one of two things is almost bound to happen: either someone else will step into the vacuum that your indecision leaves – maybe making the 'wrong' decisions, almost certainly going where you do not want to go – or else the whole business will simply lie down and die. In either case, there will be losers.

Given the reservations expressed above about trying to inculcate leadership in the space of a small specialist text, the suggestions that follow are not presumptuous attempts to preach any form of leadership gospel. They are observations about what may have a beneficial effect on the health of a business and what, if neglected, will certainly cost it dearly.

Prevailing circumstances will often have a bearing on an action or a technique when applied to a particular resource. (In other words you have to bear in mind the background context to the actions that you take.) This is especially the case where actions and techniques are applied to the management of the articulate, sentient and proud resources that constitute the staff of a business. More than that of any other piece of advice given in this book, the application of these suggestions should be introduced judiciously and with sensitivity to the effects on the individuals concerned.

Some ways of dealing with people will work only for certain character types and a misjudgement of what will and will not work will undoubtedly cause further problems. Because so much is dependent upon individual circumstances and individual people it is pointless to develop prescriptions; such judgements can only be made by the managers concerned in the light of actual events and particular knowledge of individual personalities.

Be that as it may as far as detailed actions about individuals are concerned, there are nevertheless some things that can be done – and should be done – to try to ensure that the general level of morale is not deadened by the continual buffeting, caused by bumping up against cash constraints, that is an inevitable characteristic of the early stages of a recovery.

The first of these is that, at one extreme, the small inner team of manager/directors who are in control of the planning of the recovery should do their best to make sure that the positive aspects of the recovery are the ones that make their way into the collective consciousness of the staff. In short, make sure that the managers don't always walk around with faces like a long wet weekend and make sure that the positive message of what is being done gets through to the staff as quickly and efficiently as possible. It is ridiculous to expect that the severity of the situation will not be known to the staff and that they can be led along blindly like donkeys, but there is no need to make the situation worse by rushing (or stumbling) around as if the world were going to end within the next twenty-four hours.

If the senior managers are all doing their jobs as if they do not believe that they are really worth doing because the inevitability of events is going to overtake them, then that attitude will very speedily communicate itself to the remainder of the staff. The gangrene of collective despair will then rapidly work its way into the business and overcome the potential of a situation that might otherwise have been salvageable given more time and a better and more positive approach to the problems.

By the same token, and at the other extreme, if the senior managers of the business all lurch around grinning insanely and behaving as if the situation were a huge joke, the remainder of the staff will rapidly conclude that things are not being taken seriously and will begin to lose confidence in the ability of the incumbent management to provide properly for the long-term health of the business. They will then vote with their feet and the business will suffer again.

A middle path between these two extremes is far more likely to bolster flagging morale – especially if supported with occasional group briefings about what is being done to improve the situation. Regular and fairly frequent briefings to all staff, when questions about what is being done to improve the situation can be fearlessly asked and honestly answered, are likely to produce a faster development of a sense of collective purpose than almost anything else. Briefings like this conducted by the senior managers are an excellent way of communicating rapidly, and across the business, the bones of a recovery plan or the special aspects of a strategy as they affect a certain group or department. They also have the benefit of helping to eliminate the chronic tendencies of all groups of people to generate fictitious explanations for prevailing or perceived circumstances when no better factual explanation is available. Rumour mills work overtime in poorly companies.

The best way of laying rumours is to counter them with the truth. Once things start to get better, don't keep the news to yourself as a group of senior managers: make sure that the word gets around the workforce. You should be conscious of the need to make sure that better news is made known just as speedily to your employees as to your bank manager and shareholders – although you must, of course, be wary of issuing good news too quickly only to have to retract optimistic statements when the passing tide turns against you again.

There is one last piece of advice to be given on the subject of maintaining morale in the face of commercial difficulty. The sea and the air have a lot in common as adversaries of the traveller. Mixing metaphors is never a good thing but perhaps, given its importance an exception can be made to this one. Remember – Worse Things Happen at Sea.

Key points

1. Don't neglect the impact of maintaining good morale inside your business. Concentration on purely the technical aspects of the recovery will leave you exposed to a situation where your key resource, your staff, is working at only partial capacity and effectiveness.

2. Don't neglect the need to provide yourself with an independent outsider – a supporter – with whom you can discuss some of the issues you are facing. At the least, discussing the issues will help to clarify your own thoughts.

3. Remember that there can be only one pilot-in-command and that someone has to make decisions about the future of the business and have those decisions prevail through into execution. The essence of good leadership is probably being willing to take the decisions no one else wishes to handle and then working your way effectively through the resulting actions that have to be undertaken.

4. Make sure that good news is spread inside the business; avoid extremes of reaction to events.

5. 'Worse things happen at sea.'

Appendix 1

Fraud

It will be evident that the incoming manager who enters on a recovery has to be critical of all that has gone before in determining what to do in order to bring the business back on to a proper course. One element of this critical approach not discussed until now is the consideration that a fraud has been committed. If everything else appears to have been conducted satisfactorily, and there is no self-evident reason for a business's problems in the market-place or its internal organisation, then it is a prime possibility that some form of fraud has taken place.

The ways in which fraud can be committed are legion – and new ones are being discovered every day! Fraud can also mean a variety of different things in a company context, from the manipulation of figures to conceal the true picture, possibly for personal gain, to the embezzlement of money so that cash is unlawfully used to someone's benefit, or the conversion of goods for the use of someone not entitled to them, or the disadvantaging of a minority shareholder, or even an offence under the Financial Services Act involving a knowingly reckless statement.

Because these different types of what the layperson might simply identify as fraud will manifest themselves in different ways, the actual discovery of why something is wrong can be very difficult – especially as the fraud might be concealed under the jumble of problems of a company already in trouble. But there are certain signs which may give clues to the existence of a fraud being committed.

At the simplest level, there is often a fundamental misunderstanding on the part of entrepreneurs about what is implied by the process of incorporation. This manifests itself in a lack of distinction between the money belonging to the company and the money that comes from the company to the owner-manager by way of salary and by dividend. Usually starting off as an innocent or simple-minded confusion, especially if the owner-manager is a sole shareholder, the situation can become acute under the right (or wrong?) circumstances. Fraud on the company – which is, after all, a legal person with its own rights and obligations – might then become a fraud on customers or suppliers.

An accounts department in a shambles offers numerous opportunities for concealment of mischief. An accountant or finance director who spends overly long hours compiling the accounts may be spending more time on concealing information than on deriving a true picture – or, less sinisterly, of course, may just be incompetent (which is a kind of fraud of its own).

A change of computing systems also offers unbounded scope for an adroit individual to pad or conceal information for their own benefit since the inevitable dislocation that occurs when information is being transferred over allows all sorts of havoc to be wreaked with accounts and cash balances.

Other signs of an embedded fraud might include a high and 'solid' stock level that does not move with levels of turnover; an exceptionally large number of supplier accounts with large balances which do not seem to vary with production; a continuing high level of overdraft when the company should be generating cash; a large number of suspense accounts with unallocated balances; or margins that are stubbornly resistant to management action to improve them.

The places to look for evidence are generally in the working capital elements of the balance sheet : cash, overdraft, debtors and creditors and especially stock. Manipulation of these can be used to conceal frauds, although the extent of the manipulation has to be increased over time if a continuing fraud is to be maintained. But there is no easy guidance as to how to ferret out a fraud – something will merely look wrong, and continue to look wrong after every sensible explanation has been tested.

Managerial fraud probably tends to crop up most often in the accounting department, since that is where the greatest scope lies for manipulation of the figures that will permit a fraud to take place. And if the fraud is to persist the active or passive connivance of someone in accounts is almost certainly required. On the shop-floor, aside from stock 'shrinkage', the most common area of fraud is in the area of time-card falsification or hour-padding. These are usually relatively easy to detect and in most cases are at comparatively low levels of value.

If a fraud is discovered the immediate question that has to be answered is what to do about it. The first action is to put an end to it, obviously. But thereafter the moral problem becomes a little more complicated. Bringing the police in to investigate may well result in books being impounded, bank accounts being frozen and protracted amounts of management time being expended in trawling over the past. The outcome of all this may be very uncertain in legal terms since fraud is notoriously difficult to prove to the satisfaction of a jury in a court of law if the case is at all complicated; but the company will almost certainly be throttled by the burden, and cost, of coping with its commercial and legal problems at the same time. A recoverable situation commercially which could have resulted in shareholder value being preserved and jobs being saved might be jeopardised by a dedicated and single-minded pursuit of a wrongdoer which turns out to bring no real benefit other than a moral satisfaction.

That might be considered to be a satisfactory outcome in its own right. But in the practical world, there is little gained if the innocent and the guilty are punished together. A wider purpose *might* be served by not bringing the ponderous retribution of the law into play. There is no easy or succinct advice that can be given when fraud is discovered in a company but perhaps the following rule of thumb might be applied. Where the fraud is 'internal' – affects only the internal workings of the company – or where the fraud does not involve embezzlement, then perhaps the decision not to pursue deserves a more weighty consideration. Where the fraud involves the loss of money to customers or suppliers then it probably should be brought to the attention of the police.

In either case, the discoverer must be very careful not to become an accomplice of the person who committed the original fraud, especially if the fraud has had the effect of cheating the Inland Revenue or Customs and Excise. In these instances there is no other course of action to be adopted but to disclose the problem and ensure that the identity of the guilty is isolated so that the innocent are not involved by becoming accomplices after the fact.

Appendix 2

Report format for management information

Set out below are some representative formats for the display of management information – one of the subjects discussed in Chapter 9.

The information format shown is taken from real companies but the data are made up.

The first set of information (Figs. 1–4) shows the record of turnover for a company with three divisions. The company (which also displays costs on the same basis, which is not shown here) presents the information both graphically and numerically as a matter of course. If the two formats are compared it is easy to see that the information can be better assimilated graphically. Graphs are unbeatable for displaying movements in data over a period of time. The provision of the numbers to accompany the graphs allow those discussing and reviewing the information to go into greater detail if they wish to talk about particular aspects.

The upshot is that the provision of information in such a manner enables rapid appreciation of trends, so that more time is spent in profitable analysis and less unprofitably trying to determine what is actually being shown.

Figs. 6–13 show how complex managerial accounts information can be reduced to a simple visual format that conveys easily what a complicated tabular format would have difficulty doing.

Examples of more detailed analyses of individual branch, factory or shop performance are shown below (Fig. 5). The numerical information on these graphs used to take up seven sheets of closely-typed numbers, and proved virtually impossible to analyse without much lengthy discussion, often confused and confusing.

Detailed comparison of the performance of a number of individual branches or product lines is extremely difficult without resorting to graphs. Holding so much information in your mind at any one time is a complex feat, and the juggling of two or three sets of information becomes a very difficult mental task – so difficult that you tend to concentrate on the task rather than the result and are very likely to make mistakes.

Even simple graphs can tell a vivid story. The graphical representation of break-even turnover against actual levels of turnover shown below (Fig. 14) illustrates the need for urgent management action to reduce overhead costs substantially, or to push margins up while increasing turnover.

XYZ Co Ltd – consolidated management accounts

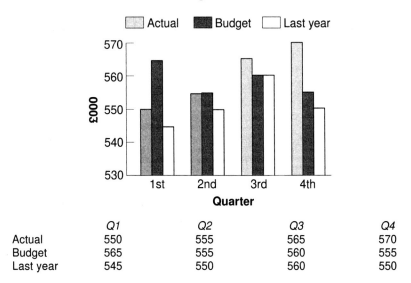

	Q1	Q2	Q3	Q4
Actual	550	555	565	570
Budget	565	555	560	555
Last year	545	550	560	550

Figure 1   Income – clickers division

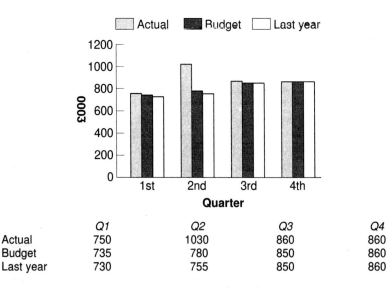

	Q1	Q2	Q3	Q4
Actual	750	1030	860	860
Budget	735	780	850	860
Last year	730	755	850	860

Figure 2   Income – widgets division

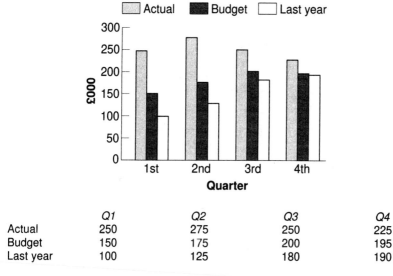

	Q1	Q2	Q3	Q4
Actual	250	275	250	225
Budget	150	175	200	195
Last year	100	125	180	190

Figure 3   Income – sprockets division

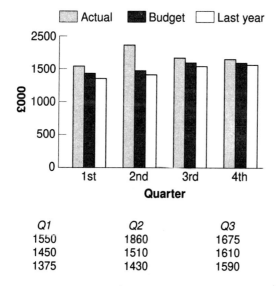

	Q1	Q2	Q3	Q4
Actual	1550	1860	1675	1655
Budget	1450	1510	1610	1810
Last year	1375	1430	1590	1600

Figure 4   Total income – all divisions

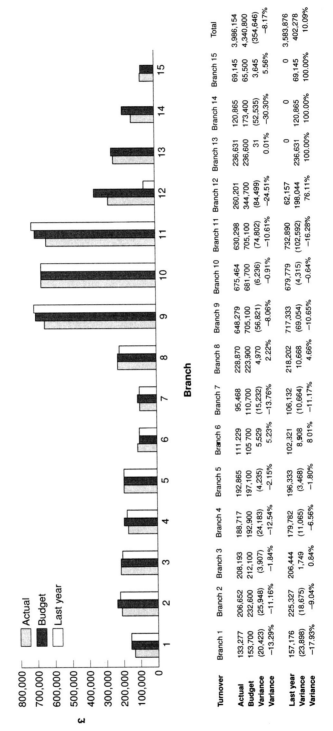

Turnover	Branch 1	Branch 2	Branch 3	Branch 4	Branch 5	Branch 6	Branch 7	Branch 8	Branch 9	Branch 10	Branch 11	Branch 12	Branch 13	Branch 14	Branch 15	Total
Actual	133,277	206,652	208,193	188,717	192,865	111,229	95,468	228,870	648,279	675,464	630,298	260,201	236,631	120,865	69,145	3,986,154
Budget	153,700	232,600	212,100	192,900	197,100	105,700	110,700	223,900	705,100	681,700	705,100	344,700	236,600	173,400	65,500	4,340,800
Variance	(20,423)	(25,948)	(3,907)	(24,183)	(4,235)	5,529	(15,232)	4,970	(56,821)	(6,236)	(74,802)	(84,499)	31	(52,535)	3,645	(354,646)
Variance	−13.29%	−11.16%	−1.84%	−12.54%	−2.15%	5.23%	−13.76%	2.22%	−8.06%	−0.91%	−10.61%	−24.51%	0.01%	−30.30%	5.56%	−8.17%
Last year	157,176	225,327	206,444	179,782	196,333	102,321	106,132	218,202	717,333	679,779	732,890	62,157	236,631	0	0	3,583,876
Variance	(23,898)	(18,675)	1,749	(11,065)	(3,468)	8,908	(10,664)	10,668	(69,054)	(4,315)	(102,592)	198,044	236,631	120,865	69,145	402,278
Variance	−17.93%	−9.04%	0.84%	−6.56%	−1.80%	8.01%	−11.17%	4.66%	−10.65%	−0.64%	−16.28%	76.11%	100.00%	100.00%	100.00%	10.09%

Figure 5 Turnover comparisons – YTD

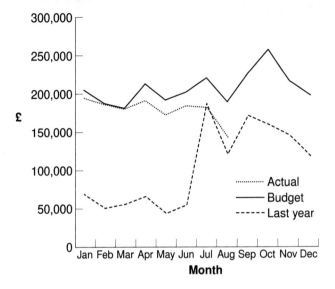

Figure 6   Gross profit month by month

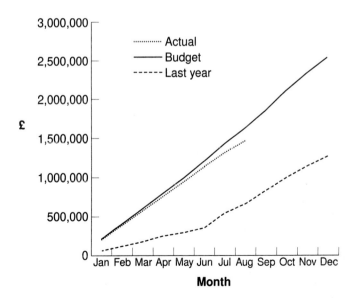

Figure 7   YTD gross profit

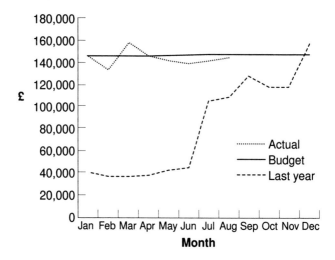

Figure 8   Branch overheads month on month

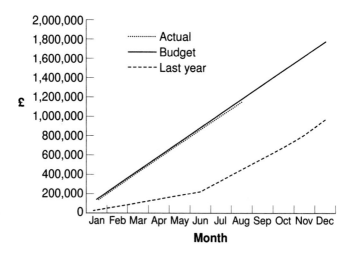

Figure 9   Branch overheads YTD

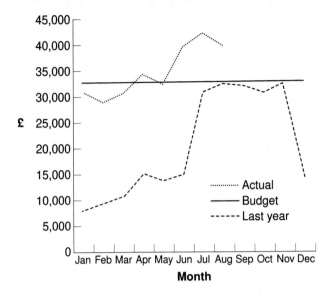

Figure 10   Administration and selling overheads month on month

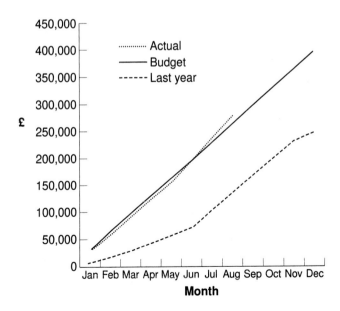

Figure 11   Administration and selling overheads YTD

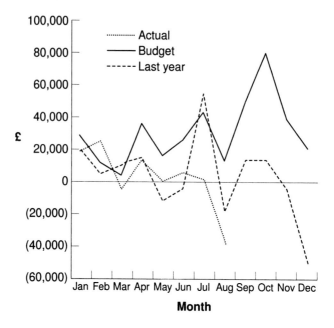

Figure 12   Trading profit month on month

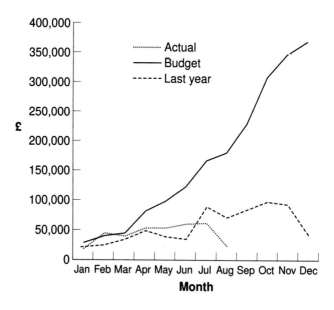

Figure 13   Trading profit YTD

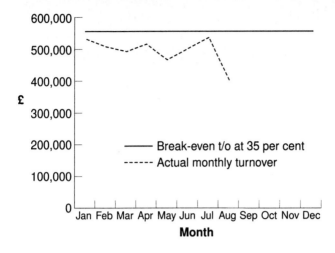

Figure 14   Turnover break-even analysis at 35 per cent contribution

Appendix 3

Confusing accounting

One of the major initial causes of financial problems in companies is bad accounting. This appendix sets out a rough description of some of the more common types of these failings likely to be encountered by someone charged with bringing a company back to financial health. Accounts formats and accounting practices should be scrutinised very early on in the recovery by the incoming manager since this is a fruitful area for quick identification of a problem. This chapter is not intended to be an exhaustive guide but is a quick reference to the simpler forms of confusion – innocent or deliberate —that may be met.

Nor is it a detailed examination of the the accounting treatment of the problems – merely a brief guide to identifying the point after isolating initial symptoms. For more detailed information, the reader should refer to the list of specialised texts in the bibliography.

In all of these areas, it will become abundantly clear that while profit can be made to lie with very little effort, the cash statement tells the truth. The recovery manager's job is not to perform a forensic investigation for the sake of ensuring that truth and justice prevail in a wicked world but to adjust the recording of information within the business so that it reflects accurately what appears to be happening and promotes the better management of the company.

While accounting problems, once identified, may appear to be the totality of problem, it must also be remembered that solving the visible mechanics is not necessarily solving the problem in its entirety. For instance, the fact that accounts are collected in a certain way which does not give accurate information for management decision-making may mean that there is a deeper *operational* problem which has to be tackled in order to fully eradicate the *information* problem. It could be that the accounts are only capable of producing rubbish because the operations are set up in such a way that the true information is not obtainable. This is often the case where physical stock control is not good, where ordering, purchasing or stock documentation is inadequate or where staff have not been properly trained in their task or in the importance of observing record-keeping procedures.

The accounting problems usually fall into one of four distinct categories:

- simple ignorance;
- self-delusion (possibly allied to laziness);
- deliberate massaging of the numbers for cosmetic purposes (a close relative of self-delusion and one which often uses the same techniques);
- fraud.

Fraud, the most serious and least tractable of these conditions, was dealt with in Appendix 1. It throws up moral problems of its own that deserve thorough consideration.

The easiest problems to identify – and sometimes to overcome – are those brought about by simple ignorance. This usually occurs in smaller companies where the owners are their own accountants, either because they started off the business doing the books and have continued to do them oblivious to the fact that the complexity of the accounting overcame their modest book-keeping skills long ago, or because they have resisted the sense of bringing in outside professional help in order 'to keep control' of the business. That is, of course, the first mistake: 'keeping control' for too long means inevitable, eventual loss of control.

This particular failing usually manifests itself in one of three ways:

1. a gradual entangling of the accounts;
2. absence of crucial pieces of information from the accounts or inaccuracy over concepts;
3. a confusion between cash and profits or even an absence of a proper predictive cashflow.

The first of these gives rise to a serpentine twisting of the numbers that takes far too much time to unravel to be of any practical use for management decision-taking and produces no sensible information when it is unravelled. In the second case, the significance of certain pieces of information is lost on the untutored book-keeper, leading to deep-seated underlying problems which pop up in other parts of the business. For instance, the importance of an accurate depreciation policy to assist in determining pricing in manufacturing industry is a minefield which even some accountants seem unable to grasp properly, never mind self-taught finance directors of small businesses.

By far the most common deficiency, though, is failing to make a proper distinction between cash and profit in the cashflow. This gives rise to endless and immediate problems in controlling outgoings against inflows. This in turn leads to serious problems that rapidly develop in intensity so that progressively greater variations from the anticipated position are experienced, which then give rise to greater and greater bewilderment.

This last situation is often experienced where the company has managed to survive without a substantial overdraft and the detailed scrutiny of management accounts that that arrangement usually brings with it. The fall, when it comes, then seems even steeper, and since the management accounts and business plan will be founded on false premises, securing borrowing to ease the situation will be even more difficult.

The solution to this sort of problem is usually fairly readily identifiable and not too difficult to implement. It involves, at its simplest, shifting the book-keeping into safer hands, disentangling the accounts and forecasts and holding tight while the problem works its way through the system. Needless to say, while this suggested remedy sounds simple in theory, it is often fraught with the most difficult sort of problem to overcome in practice – personality issues – even if the time and money is available to effect the change.

The problems brought about by self-delusion are less easy to deal with since the perpetrators know that what they are doing is wrong but have chosen to do it anyway since they want to insulate themselves from reality. Reinstalling reality into the business is no easy task, especially since this problem is usually found in businesses which are very heavily dependent on a high level of turnover (i.e. low margin) to keep themselves above water.

While the break between reality and aspiration in small businesses is usually found most glaringly in consistently high forecasts, with over-optimistic assumptions, larger businesses provide greater and wider opportunities for it to be manifested in other, more subtle ways. A firm with a large number of private shareholders or one dominant financial institution as shareholder, about to require a refinancing for instance, may attempt to adjust numbers to present a better picture than prudence would dictate. There are numerous ways to do this.

Companies which have holdings in associated companies have been known to make 'sales' on which 'profits' can be rung up for the year end by pushing out to the associates what ordinary (honest) accountants would call stock and would therefore hold in the parent company's accounts. Provided the associate goes on to sell that stock, a sale can legitimately be recorded – although the timing might be slightly skew-whiff, of course, and the associate may not be able to sell on at a further profit. (But since associate accounts are not grouped, that's the associate's problem, isn't it?)

In the even shorter term, the profit and loss account can be made to look a lot better temporarily by taking into stock the labour element of work uncompleted at the month end, at the full chargeout rate for labour (see also Chapter 9). This avenue is more than simple profit flattering and is usually the precursor to full-blown fraud since it allows all sorts of further escapades with the balance sheet.

The simplest deceit is that brought about by a change of accounting policies. By its very nature this is mostly used to enhance what might otherwise be unflattering comparisons between competitor companies in the same sector, or to produce a new basis of profit flattery for the longer term rather than a continual titivation of the profit record. For instance, changing the depreciation periods on a company's assets can have a dramatic effect on the profit and loss account – but, to be fair, this can only be done once before readers of the accounts will begin to get suspicious. However, tampering with the residual value of items subject to depreciation allows much greater scope for the application of judgement since this can also directly and substantially affect the depreciation rates charged to the P&L and, subsequently, calculations of the taxation consequences and benefits of disposal.

Readjustments of accounting policies are usually undertaken for some cosmetic reason and multiple readjustments carry a very sinister suggestion as far as the long-term truthfulness of the accounts is concerned. However, businesses which have been demerged or sold off from larger groups may well find that they have to alter their accounting policies to suit their own circumstances better now that they are out from under the wing – and the shadow – of a parent. In these circumstances, management faced with a change from what they are familiar with may well not be able to grasp the full importance of a change in accounting practice for the way they should run the business.

Groups need to harmonise their individual company policies so that there are no accounting policy variations when the accounts are grouped. This may lead to the adoption of some accounting policies which are a slightly squashed fit as far as individual subsidiaries are concerned. Once these requirements are eliminated then the businesses will have to change their requirements to match their own circumstances better.

The materiality rules can alter very dramatically for a bought-out company, for instance, when it begins to set its own accounting policies. This may have substantial implications for the way that managers think about stock control and stock valuation, depreciation policies and product costing. The recovery manager will have to add this factor into the assessment of the situation when dealing with the suitability of the management information system for the needs of the business while it is going though recovery and beyond.

Returning to the shenanigans that can be deliberately employed to camouflage a business's performance, the point at which income is recognised is another favourite which can be used for making the company's profit record seem better than it is. For example, by taking profits at the point when stage payments are made, in a business with a lengthy production cycle it would be possible for one company to produce a very much better and more consistent profit performance than a competitor who took a more cautious but lumpier view about profits and recorded them only when a project was completed.

Equally, making some provision for warranty costs in capital projects as you go along is the prudent way of doing things, but it may be discarded by an aggressive management who do not want to spoil a smartly rising profit record or perhaps, equally importantly in their own eyes, do not want to display to the world at large that they have misgivings (however prudent these may be) about their ability to complete jobs without fault.

The treatment of deferrals and accruals generally is one that should be scrutinised with care by the incoming recovery manager since this is an area often poorly handled by semi-trained accounts staff. Variations in each of these can erroneously indicate severe profit problems or suggest that things are very much better than they are, and they have the unfortunate characteristic that they are difficult to track through movements in cash.

The allied area of bad debt provision is one that should also be treated with caution. Overprovision may be just as imprudent as underprovision or disregarding the possibility of a serious bad debt affecting the business. There is an apparent tendency among many accountants in small companies to squirrel away bits of provisions so that they can bring them out later to redress the balance when things start to go wrong. This approach to accounting is pernicious in that it does not reveal an accurate picture month by month as the year unrolls. If the provision is overzealous then the profitability of the business is apparently depressed, which may result in overhasty 'corrective' action that was in fact not required at all and may then bring about unwarranted problems with future sales levels.

Other fruitful areas for consideration in trying to ferret out where mistakes may have arisen are the treatment of goodwill on past acquisitions; the treatment of exceptional and extraordinary costs; and the treatment of R&D expenditure. The abuse of goodwill has been severely clamped down on by the accounting profession's self-regulation after the surge of activity during the early 1990s but abuses are still possible.

No such controls can be applied to the distinction between extraordinary and exceptional items. The latitude allowed in deciding into which categories profits and losses made outside the normal run of business fall is very wide – it might almost be said that it is exceptional and extraordinary. The outcome of this is that managers are effectively allowed to decide whether the profit and loss account should bear the responsibility for their actions in any given year almost without regard for whether any form of consistency is maintained. Not surprisingly, since people are rarely willing to accept responsibility for the bad but are only too happy to accept the benefits of good fortune if they can get away with it, the decision-making process is open to abuse. Managers usually take credit for the good by incorporating it as an exceptional item, positioning it above the pretax line, and shrug off the bad as being beyond their control, relegating it to the extraordinary, below the pretax line.

The abuse of the accounting treatment of R&D expenditure reached such epic proportions in the case of the manufacture of aero engines that it caused the demise of the Rolls-Royce company as long ago as the 1970s. The RB211 engine took longer to get beyond prototype stage and more money to develop than had ever been contemplated, although it appeared that it would be a very successful product (a belief which time and subsequent sales have vindicated). In consequence, the costs of researching and developing the engine were taken to the balance sheet *as an asset* since they were taken to represent the real value of the effort expended on the engine which could be recovered over time. (Note how close this is to the treatment of taking labour at chargeout rate into stock, as discussed in Chapter 9.) Profits therefore remained unaffected by the huge costs of development and the management of the company deluded themselves into thinking that if profits were there then everything else must be all right, too. Cash told a different story and cash won.

Small companies and foreign currency sales are often a combustible mixture, not simply because of the normal problems of administration that any exporter or importer faces but also because of the additional problems of dealing with a different means of exchange. Accounting for foreign currency can pose any number of difficulties. The method of accounting chosen can produce great variation in the recording of profits – particularly if the goods being traded in are counted in currencies which are volatile with respect to each other. Taking the currency at spot price will probably produce very different results from the average price over a trading period, and taking the currency value to be applied to all transactions at month-end or year-end value might produce even wilder swoops in apparent profitability. Yet unless every single transaction is to be valued individually, some form of arbitrary valuation has to be applied for the purposes both of costing and of recording profit. And individual valuation will be impractical anyway where goods take some length of time to produce and the date of ordering and the date of completion are separated in time by weeks or even months.

In such a situation it is even more important that cash is treated as the only inviolable measure of performance and that profit is treated as a supportive measure of achievement rather than the primary guide.

But perhaps the biggest minefield of all – with the exception of the last item considered below, which is an exceptional case – is that of stock. Stock is the black hole of the accounting firmament. A clever or unscrupulous accountant can make the accounts show a completely different picture from reality if they are able to manipulate the stock figure. The reason for this is that since stock is the only item to appear in both P&L and balance sheet it gives the link into both records by which both can be made to appear to agree with each other.

The opportunities for manipulation are increased because of the nature of stock. It is a physical quantity to which a monetary value has to be applied; it has a time-related value; and it is usually a combination of a number of different types. Stock valuation is open to all sorts of defects, from simple omission, through mistaken counting, to arithmetic error, to deliberate under- or over-statement. The prices used to value stock are also open to misapplication since they may well be out of date or have gaps. The task of counting has to be completed quickly and the ordinary stock managers in a small business are probably too few in number so that other staff have to be drafted in to help with the task.

In addition to all this, every business has stock in its inventory which is slow-moving but still useful; stock which is damaged but still salvageable; stock which is part raw material and part manufactured: and stock which is items awaiting despatch. The part-manufactured items are themselves a combination of cost, conversion cost (labour costs and overhead) and (potential) profit. Stock is therefore not one thing but has very many types. To each of these different types should be assigned individual values to get the total value. Some of these values are not easily calculated or are calculated according to certain conventions – First In, First Out; Last In, First Out; average cost and so on.

So it should be obvious that the variations that can be played on accounts presentation by an accountant with a thorough understanding of the impact of stock movements are many in number. If the accounts do not appear to show a logical picture that squares with a company's cash circumstances, the recovery manager should look in the stock records first in order to unearth problems. If there is no explanation immediately visible then the chances are that some other areas directly linked to stock are not being recorded properly. Margins, for instance, can be verified by utilising stock records – provided that they are accurate, of course. If you discover in burrowing deeper into the problem that they are not accurate then you may have uncovered the root of the problem – or it may just be a manifestation of something more serious.

The final place to look for trouble in accounts and accounting systems is in depot and branch operations. Unless run diligently and scrupulously these can provide enormous scope for distorting the financial picture of a parent operation. Stories of branch managers who ran Ferraris and Porsches because they also ran branch accounts are far from being urban myths. As a minimum, supervision of stock counts and internal audits should always be completed by another branch manager, and on a rotational basis if that is possible, so that no mutual back-scratching can be done.

Before we conclude this section it is worth bearing in mind that there is also a sort of reverse camouflage that occurs when a company goes through a bad patch. The ditching of everything that can legitimately be thrown into a bad year may well have the effect of flattering the subsequent year's profits, but in addition has the beneficial effect of enabling the maximum recovery of corporation tax paid over in past years. This can be a worthwhile addition to a company's cashflow at a difficult time if previous tax payments were substantial and current losses also look like being substantial.

As a final warning, the recovery manager should not assume that the existence of an audit certificate is also evidence that an audit has been performed – still less that it was performed diligently. The accountancy profession is no different from any other in that it has unscrupulous practitioners who are happy to promote their clients' wealth (and of course their own) at the expense of turning a blind eye to the more irksome of accounting standards and audit requirements. Passing a professional examination does not bestow a higher sense of morality and there is no certainty that the audit partners of the regional office of a well-known accounting name will have a better grasp or sense of right and wrong than a small practice run by a single practitioner.

Appendix 4

Directors' responsibilities and disqualification

This appendix is intended as a guide only and cannot replace proper professional advice tailored to particular circumstances.

The Company Directors Disqualification Act 1986 requires receivers and insolvency practitioners to make a report to the Secretary of State for Industry, within six months of completing the receivership or winding-up of a business, on the conduct of the directors who were in charge of the company at the time it went into receivership. The court must make an order if it is satisfied that the conduct of the director makes them unfit to be involved in the management of a company. The grounds for disqualification are thus in practical terms set by the conduct of the directors themselves but commonly cited reasons for pursuit of disqualification orders are:

1. insolvent trading;
2. failure to keep proper records;
3. successive insolvencies;
4. preferring certain creditors;
5. persistent failure to file accounts.

The list of matters which must be taken into account by the court when a disqualification order is sought includes the following:

1. misfeasance or breach of fiduciary duty;
2. responsibility for non-compliance with Companies Act requirements;
3. responsibility for insolvency of a company;
4. non-cooperation with the liquidator.

If the evidence appears to suggest that there was mischief of some sort, then a disqualification order must be made. This bars a person from being a company director for a minimum of two years and a maximum of 15 years and is therefore a significant penalty. In recent years there has been a harsher attitude towards disqualifications – probably brought about by some of the well-publicised excesses of directors' behaviour in the 1980s and early 1990s.

In order for a disqualification order to be made, both the receiver and the Disqualification Unit of the Department of Trade and Industry have to agree there is a good case for the future protection of the public. Given this require-ment most applications for disqualification usually do result in an order being made. But not every time. A significant body of case law is now building up around disqualification orders since they are often appealed by those against whom they are made. But the threat of disqualification is a real one none the less for those involved in dealing with companies in trouble.

If sufficient mitigating factors exist in the individual case, it may be possible to appeal successfully. Good professional advice must be sought to determine the chances of successfully contesting the application. Not surprisingly, insolvent trading is the most frequently cited cause for an application being sought. However, while insolvent trading – trading while unable to meet debts as they fall due, according to the strict definition – is an offence under the Companies Act, the *degree* of insolvency is probably the deciding factor in determining when a director should be barred, since otherwise all companies in trouble would immediately fold without further question. The courts may offer a sympathetic hearing to directors if the circumstances surrounding the particular cases are not clear-cut. Mitigating factors may include:

1. lack of dishonest intent on the part of the directors involved;
2. loss of personal money in the company;
3. absence of any direct personal gain causing the collapse, such as excessive remuneration;
4. reliance on professional advice;
5. degree of effort applied to recover the situation.

The courts are prepared to go some way in weeding out the deliberately mischievous or incompetent from those who have merely failed to retrieve a poor situation. In a 1989 case *Re CU Fittings Ltd* Justice Hoffman said that 'a dis-passionate mind would have reached the conclusion that the company was doomed. But the directors immersed in the day-to-day task of trying to keep their company afloat cannot be expected to have wholly dispassionate minds.'

Commercial misjudgement is not usually sufficient grounds to have a director barred: a sustained period of incompetence or a deliberate breach of morality appear to be required rather than a single act of poor judgement. However, all directors are held to be competent when it comes to a company's financial position and the claim that others were concerned with the general financial state of the company is not a valid defence.

A supplementary area that directors should be aware of concerning supplied materials is governed by the application of the Romalpa doctrine (as with all the detail in this appendix, readers should consult either a good textbook or their legal advisers for the full details of the case). Briefly, the doctrine lays down the rules concerning the treatment of goods supplied to a business which have been subsequently used in the manufacturing process. When goods have been supplied to a business and have not been subsequently paid for, have not been used and are still recognisable as the materials supplied, then the creditor has the right to take them back in cancellation of the debt, if title has not passed, even though to do so may severely inconvenience the supplied company. The creditor may *not* take them back if they have already been incorporated into the manu-facturing process in some way even though they may be identifiable as supplied components. This is to protect the interest of all creditors who might be able to expect recovery of their money if a manufactured item was allowed to be sold rather than broken up by individual creditors anxious to recover goods against debts outstanding.

An example might help to illustrate the principle: a shoe manufacturer buys in laces for its shoes and owes its supplier for them; the supplier could come back to recover the laces in settlement of the debt if they had not been put into the shoes (provided that title had not passed under the terms of the contract between the two), but could not recover them if they had been placed in the shoes preparatory to them being sent to the shoe shop for sale to raise money to pay the suppliers of the leather and the polish used in the shoes as well.

Appendix 5

Checklist of ten invalid arguments with appropriate counter-arguments

1. We've always done it this way

This is no argument at all, merely an excuse for avoiding some of the tedious or arduous work involved in setting up a new system. Proponents of this line of argument probably ought to go since they are obviously appalled at the prospect of hard work and probably unwilling to exert themselves sufficiently to save their own job or those of their colleagues.

Rebuttal: AND UNTIL NOW IT'S ALWAYS BEEN DONE WRONG – LOOK AT THE SITUATION WE FIND OURSELVES IN

2. We must keep it; it makes a contribution to overheads

This argument is superficially seductive in that it suggests that the business or division or line makes profits. It is more likely that it is being advanced as a way of protecting vested interests, retaining an empire or as a device for concealing past mistakes. The true measure of whether an activity should be retained is whether it makes profits after all attributable charges have been levied against it.

Rebuttals: *either* THE CONTRIBUTION TO OVERHEADS IS LOST AFTER ATTRIBUTABLE COSTS ARE INCLUDED AND SO IT GOES *or* BUT IT DOES NOT FIT WITH OUR PLANS FOR THE FUTURE AND SO IT GOES *or (if all else fails)* IT GOES OR YOU GO

3. The accounts department won't stand for that

This again is no argument at all. The basic rule comes into operation here: there is only one pilot-in-command. Accounts staff – even good ones – are even more replaceable than salespeople if it comes to the crunch. Make the accounts department do what you want them to do, not the other way round.

Rebuttal: THE ACCOUNTS DEPARTMENT WILL DO AS THEY ARE TOLD

4. We need to keep this level of stock in case . . .

This argument is always used by the Klingons – not Captain Kirk's arch-enemies but the people who want to cling on to stock as some form of comfort factor. The argument has any number of subsidiary clauses none of which are valid. Let your suppliers hold stock – you want the cash it represents.

Rebuttal: STOCK IS CASH UNDER ANOTHER NAME

5. I can't cut my salary

This one has to be treated with a little more caution than simply being refuted out of hand. For instance, it is unreasonable to expect employees on £10,000 a year to reduce their salary since they are being asked to make a sacrifice that will cost them a great deal for the ultimate benefit of the shareholders. Why should they? But people in a senior position – a shareholding managing director, say, on £35,000, with a large house, a company car, pension benefits and health insurance paid by the company – ought to be invited to consider the options more carefully before they nail their remuneration colours to the mast. They probably have the capacity to reduce their expenditures or borrow to cover inescapable outgoings, even though each of those may be temporarily unpalatable.

Rebuttal: THE CHOICE IS TO CUT YOUR SALARY OR DO WITHOUT ONE ENTIRELY

6. We have to have company cars

Another mostly unfounded argument. But, unfortunately, company cars cause more problems than any other aspect of company administration. Any management which values its perk of cheap transport above its employment probably does not deserve to be saved. There is some justification for this argument being employed where the company managers are essentially salespeople who travel long distances regularly, but there is little real justification for the accounts director or the MD or the company secretary to have a company car other than that they are keeping up with the others.

Rebuttal: THERE WILL BE NO COMPANY CARS AT ALL IF THERE IS NO COMPANY

7. We know what's going on in our market-place, we don't need any more information

The blinkered sales director usually employs this one since they are determined not to waste money on market information and let good information get in the way of their prejudices. It may be true in certain circumstances that there is little to be gained from expensive, tailored market research or formal bought-in market reports. But better marketing information does not have to cost money. The business's own sales force is probably the best source of market information available in terms of knowing what the customer really wants, so long as they are encouraged to ask the right questions and then accurately relay the information back.

Rebuttal: THEN WHY ARE OUR COMPETITORS STILL DOING WELL?

8. We shouldn't tell the workforce what is going on, it will unsettle them

Treating your workforce like any other dumb asset is not the way to get the best out of them. True, some information of a confidential nature has to be confined to those who have to know. But much information that should be in the hands of employees in a recovery is needlessly kept from them. The workforce in many businesses is an untapped resource, which – if brought on-side – could transform the potential of many areas of the operation.

Rebuttal: RUMOURS BASED ON INCORRECT SUPPOSITION ARE FAR MORE UNSETTLING THAN GOOD INFORMATION SENSITIVELY PASSED ON

9. We can't improve cash collection any further

Usually incorrect but not always so. Cash collection can usually be improved if adequate effort is devoted to it at a senior level. For this argument to hold water a reducing number of debtor days ought to be proveable. If not, the rebuttal is simple.

Rebuttal: TREAT THE CASH OWED TO THE COMPANY AS IF IT WERE YOUR OWN. IF YOU NEEDED THE MONEY AS BADLY AS THE COMPANY DOES, WOULD YOU LET DEBTORS CONTINUE TO HOLD YOUR MONEY?

10. We can't get rid of him, he's invaluable

Rebuttal: NO ONE IS INDISPENSABLE

Case Study 1

Company A had two divisions which turned over in total about £2.5m annually, manufacturing and selling a very wide range of products to a specialist market.

Its customers were individuals, charities, schools, other businesses and local authorities, a blue chip customer base; bad debts were very few. Cashflow was heavily uneven, as was the order book, both being strongly skewed towards the final quarter of the year, which coincided with the end of the local authorities' budgetary year. In addition, the largest single class of customers was a traditionally slow payer – but the company had been (modestly) profitably run for ten years, having been built up by the hard work of the principal shareholder and managing director, who knew the market inside out and was a respected authority in the company's field.

However, turmoil in the reorganisation of some major customers coupled with some loss of discipline in the manufacturing side of the business resulted in serious financial losses which meant the company had to seek outside financing. At the same time a new chairman, with big company experience, was brought in at the instigation of minor (family) shareholders, and with the reluctant agreement of the managing director, to assume overall strategic control.

There were considerable disparities in ability and competence between the members of the management team. Financial reporting systems, which were unsophisticated but had been adequate for the company in times of profitable trading, were insufficiently robust to cope with different terms of trade.

An over-optimistic business plan (which did, however, attract further funding), coupled with a further downturn in the market-place, increased pressure on the company. In particular, three separate ventures into slightly different markets from the core business, undertaken at the instigation of the chairman in an effort to diversify the company out of trouble, went badly wrong, increasing losses and draining cash out of the company. The continued reversal of fortunes required further financing by the outside financier to (eventually) over twice the initial investment, because the company's bankers took fright and capped the overdraft level at a position too low for the company's needs.

The absence of adequate managerial and financial resources was coupled with increasing antagonism between the new chairman and the principal shareholder as a result of a clash of personalities, with the managing director's talents becoming increasingly marginalised as the chairman sought to impose his own business methods in opposition to the culture of the company – which had contributed to the company's success. The chairman was then replaced by the outside financier, who commanded a majority of the shares following the refinancings.

A new chairman then worked with the managing director, rather than against him, to produce the following recovery plan.

Actions for recovery

Undertaken initially and simultaneously – to keep the business flying

(1) Reduce the number of goods offered for sale.
Purpose: To increase the salespeople's ability to sell competently the best margin goods – or more accurately, what were believed to be the best margin goods (since the management information could not distinguish properly) – to try to stimulate sales and cashflow. Sales training, principally internal, was given a high priority.

(2) Increase the pressure exerted on debtors.
Purpose: To increase the inflow of cash, relieving the pressure on the overdraft.

Next steps – navigating the recovery

(3) Prepare a proper business plan for each division of the company.
Purpose: To get the local management to review their activities and make corrections to the operations for which they were responsible themselves.

(4) Review the management information and its collection.
Purpose: To begin to map out the recovery strategy by finding out where the problems lay.

(5) Undertake a review of stock holdings.
Purpose: To bring stocks back into line with the new (reduced) product range; to reduce cash outflow by cutting back on stock replacement.

(6) Review manufacturing processes.
Purpose: Restoration of sound manufacturing practices, reduction of stock levels, elimination of excess cost.

Implementing the recovery – communicating the new course

(7) Reduce the headcount in all areas of the business to essential staff only, following the reviews detailed above.
Purpose: To reduce the costs of the business to a level more appropriate to sales income to minimise the outflow of cash.

(8) Reinvigorate sales and marketing functions.
     Purpose: First to re-engage the energies of the managing director/principal share-holder, the member of the management team who had the best perception of the market-place that the company served; and second, to provide for new products to restore the company's position in the market-place.

(9) Let the bank know what is being done.
     Purpose: To ensure that there were no more misunderstandings over trading health resulting in further cash problems once the new course had been embarked upon.

Final steps – heading for the destination

(10) Reorganise the managerial team to support the new objectives.

Result

Within a year the company had turned round from losses of roughly £200,000 annually to a profit of £50,000; profitability continued to rise (but not without incident) thereafter, both as a proportion of turnover and absolutely; the market position was restored; very successful new products were launched; the sales team settled down and became very successful at effectively selling high-margin goods that required a sophisticated and expert selling approach; the size of the range of products was gradually restored in a controlled way.

Notes from a strategy meeting, March 1993

MAJOR CONCLUSIONS

This note sets out the major conclusions that we reached at the meeting we held on Tuesday 9th March.

I have also set out on a separate sheet some of the side issues that were raised in order to amplify the thinking that went behind the discussion leading to the conclusions which we reached.

As we all agreed the next stage is for us to gather again on Tuesday 30th March at 9am to try to hammer out a strategy following on from our examination of the business.

To this end, it might be useful – as has been suggested – if we all come armed with some prepared contributions; attached to this sheet are some suggested areas, that individuals might like to consider, on the implications of our discussions for a strategic view of their own areas of activity.

OVERALL SWOT ANALYSIS: STRENGTHS

1. Expertise in individual functional areas; there are people in the business who know what they are doing and do it well.
2. Brand value; the name stands for something and has some meaning to customers.
3. The commitment and hard work of staff in a generally supportive workforce.
4. The range of products offered by the company; there are solutions to most problems encountered by customers within the product range.
5. Flexibility; the company and its workforce can accommodate different working conditions and demands.
6. Design strength; few other companies can field a design process like ours for a range of products.
7. Market appreciation; we have a good sense of the market for our range of products because of our organisational set-up and the inherent abilities of our design and marketing functions.
8. Service level; the standard of our service to customers – while capable of improvement – is better than that of our competitors.

OVERALL SWOT ANALYSIS: WEAKNESSES

1. There is a serious lack of adequate management information throughout the business but especially about our market-place.
2. There has been a lack of consistent managerial policy over the past three years (at least).
3. There has been an absence of successful new products over the past two years.
4. The balance sheet is weak and will hamstring fast recovery managerially as well as financially.
5. There has been a flip-flop product and marketing strategy over the past three years.
6. Marketing has been neglected as a function.
7. Production control is poor.
8. The sales office is an Achilles' heel.
9. Our resources are spread very thin.
10. We are overly reliant on key people.
11. The state, size and layout of our premises are a serious potential inhibition to our future growth.
12. Our strategic stockholding/purchasing is poor.

OVERALL SWOT ANALYSIS: OPPORTUNITIES

1. Our core activities are in growth markets.
2. The company is now financially stable – more or less. It is at least back in profit and making inroads into accumulated losses.
3. There has been and is a continuing redefinition of our purpose and strategies which could bring substantial financial and commercial benefits.
4. We now have a chance to apply the lessons we learned since we are still here.

OVERALL SWOT ANALYSIS: THREATS

1. The activities of our competitors. Our strategic response must be linked to the conditions of the market-place.
2. Product introduction: delay would prove very costly to us.
3. Failure to review and appreciate market changes appropriately.
4. Financial changes affecting our customers which we do not yet fully appreciate.

OVERALL SWOT ANALYSIS: SUBORDINATE ISSUES

Strengths
(2) Brand value – we think that the name means something but what exactly is it? Does a stronger appreciation of this hold a key to the development of our strategy?

(4) Is the breadth of our range in fact a weakness? Are we perceived as fuzzy generalists?

(6) Do we delude ourselves about our design strength? Unless design strength can be translated into efficient manufacture and then sold to a willing buyer it is a wasted ability.

Weaknesses
The Sales Office – geography, organisation, staffing were all blamed for its problems. As the critical link in the chain we must solve the difficulty.

Is our product-costing ability sufficiently strong yet for us not to regard it as a serious weakness?

Opportunities
Our competitors are largely one-product companies as far as — goes but are very different for — . Does this imply a different form of financing or organisational arrangement between — and —?

Threats
Do we properly understand our competitors' strengths, weaknesses and so on? By exploring these we may be able to find our own best route in the market-place.

Do we adequately plan the process of introduction of our products taking into account all the variety of factors known to us: price, competitors' response, market-place change?

SUGGESTED AREAS FOR CONSIDERATION

Managing director
1. How can we improve our management information systems?
2. Will expansion be supportable financially and organisationally?
3. What is the solution to the Sales Office problem?

Operations director
1. How can we further improve efficiency?
2. What would be a sensible distribution of resources of factory and manufacturing personnel between our two operations?

3.   How can we improve our strategic stocks and purchasing while still operating with restricted cashflow? Are the two compatible or exclusive?

Sales director
1.   How can we get product/market information formalised?
2.   How can we get everyone up to the standard of John Smith?
3.   What methods can we employ to monitor our sales force efficiently?

Board
1.   Where is our major threat going to come from?
2.   How can we capitalise on our success with company A?
3.   How can we make the business stronger across a range of activities?
4.   How do we overcome supply problems?
5.   What can we do to improve our sales force ability?

Design team
1.   What should be our product strategy for the next six, twelve and eighteen months?
2.   What should be the company's major thrust – broad development of a number of products or head-on competition with specific competitors?
3.   How can design best be translated to production and then taken over to leave you to design rather than product engineer?
4.   Are we overly dependent upon one or two prototypers?
5.   What information do you need from the market-place we could provide you with?

Case Study 2

Company B was involved in the manufacture of machinery of a specialised nature. The business was the result of a merger between two companies which had been effected under particularly profitable and unusual circumstances for one of them, so that the funds borrowed by the acquiring company to make the acquisition had been paid for out of the profits of a large contract won by the acquired company just after the merger.

The share structure was unusual in consequence, with a substantial minority shareholding in the subsidiary and a single shareholder in the top company – which before the merger had been the financially weaker of the two but had the greater potential for development.

The majority shareholder was a clever engineer, whose attention was easily distracted by his many external interests. He had gathered around him a management team that was not really up to the task involved, for many different reasons, in propelling what was at root a very good medium-size engineering business in a very difficult part of the manufacturing sector.

With the decline in the economy at the end of the 1990s, the company experienced a rapid deterioration in cashflow as orders dried up for the standard machines sold by the subsidiary. Deposits from customers for the bespoke machines made by the acquiring company, which should have been used to fund the stock required for building new machines, were used instead to fund the day-to-day expenditure of the business – which sagged under the weight of frivolous expenditure on expensive cars, state-of-the-art computer-aided design equipment (which cost a small fortune to run every month and which was heavily under-utilised) and outdated working practices.

Unable to take a decision about the proper level of resources for the business, the chairman/managing director allowed the situation to drift until the bank took a firm position and reduced the overdraft progressively over a very short period of time to a level where continued trading was only barely sustainable.

Action taken to bring about recovery

Steps taken immediately – to keep the business flying

(1) Establish a regular series of meetings of the operations director, accountant and managing director to review the situation weekly. Reports to the bank on fortnightly basis.

Purpose: The company's activities were essentially long term in that the building of a bespoke machine could take several months and there was little that could be done to alter the company's trading situation immediately. Better to plan out the path with the cooperation of the senior managers than to take precipitate action – especially given the nature of the shareholding structure.

The introduction of a systematic and methodical planning process also gave the bank temporary comfort and led them to withhold any further action that could have adversely affected the business. Fortnightly reporting gave a little latitude to report some progress after every meeting of managers and also allowed a little fat to be built up so that good news could be dribbled out regularly while bad news could be withheld until events overtook it.

The sales director was not involved in the discussions both because of the need to keep the meetings tight and because the sales department had substantially under-performed; his job was therefore at risk, since the chairman could have been tasked with sales activity – at which he was very good – and the sales department disbanded.

The meetings also had the three further benefits of reducing the chairman's ability to take decisions on his own, making him accountable for actions he was tasked with and involving him in joint decisions, thereby – initially at least – making it difficult for him to subvert decisions he did not like.

Next steps – navigating the recovery

(2) Review the company's balance sheet and trading expenses.

Purpose: Any alteration in trading funds would have to be generated out of savings in expenditure and sales of assets in the short term, with the possibility of recapital-isation having to be deferred until the internally generated recovery could be demonstrated to be under way.

The company had two sets of premises and a bloated car policy based on purchase rather than leasing. Disposal of these assets in favour of renting more appropriate premises and leasing more suitable cars was an obvious source of funds since it brought in cash, reduced outgoings and gave some certainty to future expenditure.

(3) Redefine tasks of senior management.

Purpose: By defining tightly the responsibilities of each member of the management team, scope for interference, or for neglect of a task, or for overlap was theoretically minimised.

(4) Define targets for the sales team to meet as part of the refined business plan.

Purpose: Part of the problem with the sales department had been the unsystematic nature – the reactive attitude – of their activities, which had led to a lack of account-ability and no knowledge of why customers had chosen another competitor's machine when orders were lost. The imposition of basic sales disciplines improved sales information and planning (although not necessarily sales results).

Implementing the plan – communicating the new course

(5)   Inform selected trading partners of the changes that were being made.
      Purpose: The company was dependent upon the goodwill of subcontractors for many of its jobs. Some dislocation was inevitable following the implementation of changes, and prior warning and support were preferable to later explanation and excuses.

(6)   Reorganise the shareholding structure.
      Purpose: The shareholding structure was a major obstacle to the recapitalisation of the business – cleaning it up had three benefits: it made an injection easier for a financier to accomplish; it would provide less scope for the major shareholder to wriggle, to avoid accepting an injection, because of the simpler structure; and it drew to the attention of the minority shareholders their directorial responsibilities.

(7)   Overhaul the accounts system.
      Purpose: Poor accounts information was a major cause of the company's problems. Information was not collected or used effectively. Estimating was done poorly on outdated design information and designs were never frozen, so that changes were effected by the planning department during the process of building and never recosted. The chronic shortage of cash led to shortages of components, with canni-balisation of half-built machines being a regular occurrence in order to satisfy a customer's demands. The effects of such actions were never recorded by the accounting system in terms of labour hours expended on machines and never allowed for in estimating the price of new machines.
      Only by completely rebuilding the accounts system could the necessary changes be made to estimating, costing and subsequent profitability.

Result

In the event, although the path could be mapped out fairly easily, the attitudes of the chairman/managing director, the absence of any real authority that he allowed the operations director and the embedded position of the accountant – who was largely responsible for not overhauling the shortcomings of the accounts system – prevented any real changes being made to the organisation of the business or to the trading situation. The business continued to lurch along by cutting the frequency of payments to staff when cash was short – effectively making them shareholders temporarily but with none of the rights of shareholders – and by delaying payments to creditors to the utmost. The real problems of lack of profitability and insufficient capitalisation were not tackled until new owners bought the business.

Case Study 3

Company C was involved in the manufacture of capital goods, largely to customer order but with some standard designs, and had been the subject of a management buy-in/buy-out. The buying-in team had changed at the last moment, just before the deal was completed, when the designated finance director dropped out. He had suggested his successor and the new management team had accepted the candidate.

Part of the new management's business plan was to extend the range of products sold by the company into an area of the market-place where they believed there existed a gap. Despite early success in winning orders the company was unable to produce the new products successfully, for a variety of reasons, and had to undertake subcontract manufacture. This proved very costly in terms of cash since the business had had to recruit new staff to train in preparation for the new product range for which orders had been won.

Since the company had generated cash until the expansion, the new management had not organised a level of overdraft that would be sufficient to cover unexpected events. Fearing the consequences of a refinancing very soon after the original investment, the new finance director manipulated the figures presented to his colleagues at board meetings in order to conceal the true financial picture in terms of both immediate profitability and longer-term cash requirements. In consequence the company's position steadily worsened as the corrective action necessary to bring overheads back into line with turnover was deferred.

The company's order book continued to grow because of the success of the product in the market-place, while the working capital position steadily worsened. Inevitably, the manipulations required to support the faked profit and cashflow positions grew more and more extreme. No accounts staff of a calibre to work out what was going on were employed for long enough to voice the suspicions they might have developed. Eventually the fabrication of data became unsustainable as the year end approached.

By the time the finance director was dismissed from the company the accounting system was in a shambles. He had used the opportunity of the installation of a new software package to disguise his actions further and this had created havoc with costing data. The remaining management team set about repairing the damage to the accounts system while continuing to struggle against acute cash shortages and the resulting demands of creditors.

A threefold strategy was pursued:

1. to rectify the problems in the accounts system as soon as possible; this took longer than anticipated because of problems with the year-end audit;
2. to pursue the prospect of additional equity as a matter of urgency; this was held up because of problems with the year-end figures;
3. to try to minimise costs in the meantime and use the available management information to do this.

After some extended delays, additional equity was injected into the company, which gave some temporary respite from creditor pressure. However, in the meantime, as a consequence of suppliers' accounts not being paid promptly, vital components did not arrive on time, which meant that goods could not be despatched to get more money in to pay the creditors. A vicious spiral of cash starvation pulled the company deeper and deeper into problems.

The directors took professional insolvency advice. Having considered this advice, their conclusion was that by continuing to trade they would be improving the lot of individual creditors. The principal consideration in this decision was that the order book was strong and remained so despite the rumours of problems in the market-place. Carefully prepared forecasts suggested that if the company could overcome the hump of payments needed to put creditors back on roughly normal trading terms, the cash problem would rectify itself as a consequence of the bulge of orders that had been received.

Soundings were taken of creditors as to whether a Creditors Voluntary Arrangement would be an acceptable route out to try to preserve the business. This would at least offer the prospect of recovery of some of the debts due, while maintaining the existence of a continuing customer, gradually increasing in strength, to those suppliers who wished to continue trading with the company.

The time necessary to put an arrangement in place was not available since the arrangements that the company had entered into with one of its preferential creditors could not be met as a consequence of further delays in receipts caused by delayed despatches. Problems of arranging support for the CVA became insurmountable and the company went into receivership.

Key points

1. The overdraft was never fixed at a level that was adequate for the company's needs in the light of its departure into new areas of the market.

2. There was little additional security against which to balance a further overdraft allowance and so the only route out was additional equity. This is difficult to attract into a failing business.

3. Action taken to balance overheads against turnover was delayed since good accounting information was not available until the last months of the company's existence. If sufficient action had been taken earlier to reduce overheads then the outcome might have been different.

4.   Insufficient time was allowed to get the CVA in place despite there being a general willingness on the part of creditors to contemplate the procedure.

Lessons

1.   Cash availability is the key point of any rescue. Without it there is no future for any company.

2.   If in doubt, cut overheads. Forget the siren song that cutting too hard will damage the business – cut hard to take out any weak links or surplus cost. Functions and people can be replaced but lost time and cash cannot.

3.   Allow sufficient time to get a CVA in place. A *minimum* of a month is required and preferably six weeks should be allowed.

4.   The importance and significance of good accounting advice cannot be over-emphasised. The root of the problem and the company's inability to get itself out of its problems were largely due to the lack of good accounting information.

Case Study 4

Company D, in a particular area of the leisure industry, had been started by its three owner-managers after they became dissatisfied with local facilities. Each of the owner-managers had been involved in the running of the business, although none had any formal management training. One looked after the operational management; one looked after the accounts; one acted as company chairman. They had borrowed systems and best practice from the industry leaders so that as individual operations each site ran very well and was recognised as a very good example of its kind across the industry.

Unfortunately, the company was very substantially geared and all its available cash went into servicing the debts it owed, which were secured on the freehold properties belonging to it. Relationships with the local bank were strained since the deal had not been done by the local branch and there was a certain amount of not-invented-here attitude, compounded by the fact that the company struggled to make its interest payments and capital repayments despite its very strong cashflow.

Cash availability had been further weakened by a serious leakage of cash into an abortive refinancing, which had come after a very hot summer when business had dropped off as potential customers stayed outside in the sunshine. Professional fees for lawyers, surveyors and financial advisers had taken a huge chunk out of available cash and severely reduced profits. Dividend payments were being missed; the small number of small shareholders behind the two individual major shareholders were disaffected and the institutional shareholder was losing confidence in the management in consequence.

The owner-manager in charge of operations day to day struggled to control the business and was becoming overwhelmed by problems. The management of the company's affairs became entangled with the management of the individual centres. The standard of accounts information provided to the directors was poor and did not distinguish properly between cash and profit. Creditors had begun to extend ominously and there were serious delays in paying statutory creditors.

Eventually the local bank had the case taken out of its hands and the bank's recoveries branch was put in charge. Uncertain of the validity of the information they were receiving from the company, they put in a firm of investigating accountants to review the business. This firm had looked at the company in the past for the local branch and the relationship between the reporting partner and the company's directors was not a happy one.

Not surprisingly, the reporting accountants recommended that the company be put into receivership so that the bank could realise its security. Receivership was avoided only because the investing institution undertook to strengthen management and support the balance sheet if required so that the lending bank's interest and capital payments could be met.

Actions

(1) The accounts function was taken out of the hands of the ex-shareholder and given to a specialist who operated part-time and could produce reliable, accurate information in a timely fashion.

(2) Costs were reduced by displacing the chairman, who took a full salary out of the business, into a non-executive position.

(3) New cashflows were produced which properly distinguished between cash and profit, indicated the extent and incidence of the problem of cash availability and provided a reliable platform from which to work.

(4) Discussions were rapidly undertaken with the statutory creditors so that time was made available to pay the debts due and catch up with the arrears.

(5) Modest price increases were instituted which greatly improved the profitability and cash generation of the business.

(6) Responsibility for the day-to-day operations of the business was pushed back to the individual site managers, who were given budgetary discretion for some of the areas under their control and offered participation in any overall cost savings.

(7) A small number of simple management ratios were regularly collected and used to analyse the profitability of individual areas of operations of the business.

(8) The risks of the business were reduced by expanding into similar areas using methods that were not cash-hungry (taking on management contracts, for instance) and spreading the interest and capital repayment load over a wider number of similar operations.

(9) Not least, once the initial problems had been overcome, the interest and capital repayments on the (very large) loans were rescheduled across the year so that the financing burden became no more severe in any one month – although the total outflow to the bank remained the same. This greatly reduced pressure on individual month's cashflow.

Lessons

1. Confusion between cash and profitability is the single greatest factor in reducing a business to its knees. There is no substitute for proper and timely accounts information.

2. Most businesses service a market that can absorb some modest price increases which will temporarily ease the cash position. In the case of leisure businesses this effect can be very pronounced since a small price increase per unit over a large number of unit sales (admissions) can have a very significant effect.

3. Discussions with creditors – especially statutory creditors – will ease apparently insuperable cashflow problems significantly if they are undertaken early enough, are reasonably pitched and are adhered to.

4. Simple cost reductions can have beneficial effects on cashflow when cash is tight. Do not spurn the prospect of reducing outgoings, however small the reductions may be.

Case Study 5

Because of a serious decline in trading performance, which included problems in making interest and capital repayments, the company had been subjected to an accountants' investigation by its bankers. The investigation was to be conducted by a partner in the recoveries and receiverships division of the firm.

The firm selected for the investigation had been called in twice before because of trading problems experienced by the company and on each occasion quite serious friction had developed between the management of the company and the accountants over the way that information had been interpreted by the accountants, or the accuracy of the conclusions that had been reached. The particular partner nominated by the bank had been involved on each previous occasion.

Because of this unfortunate history, the accountants required that the bank institute a form of wording into the terms letter controlling the investigation that allowed the bank irrevocable authority to debit the company's overdraft in favour of the accountants for their fees, without any apparent ability on the part of the company to refuse this payment.

The managers did not attend any pre-meetings with the bank or the investigating accountants – because they were not asked to do so or did not press to do so. In consequence they were not able to plan the impact of the investigation on the company and did not have available any up-to-date forecasts for the use of the investigators at the time that they were required, since managerial activities had descended to firefighting to scrape together cash to meet day-to-day needs.

Not surprisingly, given the history of their relationship with the company's management and the chaotic nature of the management activity that they found, the accountants reached the conclusion that the managers were unable to control the business in a way that protected the bank's security and recommended that the company be put into receivership. Since they had such an intimate knowledge of the company's operations after three investigations, they also indicated their willingness to serve as receivers.

Delivery of the final version of the report to the bank was effected within minutes of the management having received a copy – although they had seen an earlier draft which had blank subsections containing information yet to be supplied by valuers employed by the accountants concerning the value of the assets against which the bank's loans were charged. The management of the company suspected that the report's conclusions had been reached before this information was available.

The bank set a date for a meeting for all parties to consider the report and the management used this time to rebut the fundamental assumptions that the accountants had deployed in arriving at the conclusions of the report. The management's detailed rebuttal was presented at the meeting. The accountants had not consulted management about these 'facts' prior to them being included in the report.

As a consequence of this work, receivership was narrowly avoided; the bank was sufficiently uncertain of the case advanced by the accountants in the face of the management's determined resistance to the report's conclusions to be unwilling to push the company over the brink.

The management then refused to pay the bill invoiced by the accountants who relied upon the bank's 'irrevocable authority'. After some protracted negotiations, during which the legal basis for such an arrangement was questioned by the management, the bank refused to execute the arrangement, preferring to wait until the company reached a settlement with the accountants.

Continuing refusal by the company to meet the accountants' bill in full resulted in an eventual settlement at 75 per cent of the invoiced amount six months after initial presentation of the invoice, when the company was finally in a position to be able to afford the impact on its cashflow.

Within ten months of the report being concluded the company had eliminated its overdraft, was exceeding its internal forecasts and received an offer from a competitor which valued it at several times its asset value.

Further advice and select bibliography

The list below sets out some of the sources of help and advice for those finding themselves in the situation of trying to rescue an ailing business.

Publications

In general, there are very few texts that deal with rescuing small companies in trouble. Management magazines and some academic reviews from the larger management schools carry occasional articles, but while these are useful they are usually of limited direct application to particular circumstances.

The most comprehensive single source of advice on the administrative practicalities of running a business is the *Company Secretarial Manual* (compiled by Keith Walmsley) published by the ICSA. This is a useful starting point for any questions concerning the administration of a business and what the law requires to be done.

Sadly, a more suitable text for private company administration, *Small Company Secretarial Practice* (ICSA) is no longer available, but it is useful if you can still find a copy. A less detailed treatment is given in *Running A Limited Company* by David Impey and Nicholas Montague (Jordans, 1994, second edition), which describes the requirements of running a limited company in a simple straightforward way, without the supporting documentation of the ICSA manual.

For the manager pitch-forked into a rescue, having little accounting knowledge, *Interpreting Company Reports and Accounts* by Holmes and Sugden (Prentice Hall Europe, 1997, sixth edition) is a simple comprehensive guide to the basics. Supplement that with *Creative Accounting* by Ian Griffiths (Sidgwick and Jackson, 1987) and the diligent manager will probably begin to feel more comfortable in getting to grips with the construction of a basic management information system, and the pitfalls that treating existing information indiscriminately can lead to.

Useful marketing, historical and ownership information on competitors can be derived from publications such as *Kompass*, *Key British Enterprises* and *Who Owns Whom*. Brief, digestible examples of useful business strategies adopted by others are given in

160

Business Wargames by Barrie G. James (Penguin, 1985). The *Financial Times* is a useful source of real life examples in its Small Companies/The Growing Business section. The *Company Secretarial Review*, which is published fortnightly, is a useful digest of the main developments in legal and regulatory matters affecting all sizes of business, and carries regular articles dealing with particular aspects of these changes.

Other sources

The comprehensive reference libraries attached to local lending libraries in most large towns, are by far the best initial sources of information on almost any aspect of business. Increasingly, these organisations have set up special business sections to cater for commercial enquiries.

Spending some time here researching the basics of an enquiry could save a great deal on the cost of a similar exercise launched through a professional adviser. Market reviews and monographs on particular aspects of market places published by ICC or Jordans should be available from such libraries.

For those within striking distance of London, the City Business Library carries an unrivalled collection of marketing information that can be searched through.

Useful contacts

The Society of Practitioners in Insolvency publish a useful leaflet which is called simply *Understanding Insolvency* and this is available free from the society at 18–19 Long Lane, London, EC1A 9HE.

Customs and Excise, Inland Revenue and Department of Social Security are all usually amenable to discussion over the short-term phasing of payments to them if they are approached soon enough, and if the phasing is over a short period. Local offices should be approached in the first instance.

Local Business Links are usually aware of the sources of limited help that can be drawn on in the short term from government departments. They are also good sources of information for published market reviews and for foreign marketing information.

Members of professional institutes should not neglect the resources that these can offer. The Institute of Directors offers a useful library service where books can be borrowed by members, and this is supplemented by a telephone advisory service.

Index